SB: 1 or God

SB: 1 or God

Everyone has the
Hidden Question

Karl Mark Maddox

VANTAGE PRESS
New York

Published by Vantage Press, Inc.
516 West 34th Street, New York, New York 10001

Manufactured in the United States of America
ISBN: 0-533-13193-6

Library of Congress Catalog Card No.: 99-93933

0 9 8 7 6 5 4 3 2

To the cool people

Contents

A Special Note

The content of *SB: 1 or God* is fictitious. There have been no encounters with any paranormals or UFOs or anything unknown. The author has selected his own name as a matter of ease in writing and to protect any innocents. *SB: 1 or God* is most likely the pinnacle of controversy concerning the religions of earth. In no way does the publisher acknowledge the content of *SB: 1.* The content is intended as a contribution to a very troubled human race. We can save ourselves if we acknowledge ourselves. *SB: 1 or God* more than acknowledges the human race. Please enjoy this science fiction, and make a contribution to Mother Earth.

—Karl Mark Maddox

SB:1 or God features an informative website at:
  http://Sites.Netscape.net/sb1orgod

Prelude: A Prior Life

"Pilot, abort . . ."

"Don't make me shut you down!"

"You are entering air space declared by the war council as a safe zone to opposing forces, should you violate this agreement our safe zone will certainly be targeted."

"You received the report as well as I did, the Midway offered complete surrender, they sent her to the bottom, computer I command over ride S111x."

"Cannot override, you have violated air space and you have not been engaged."

"Shut down sequence, main processor, backup systems, here goes the switch C21, you're outa here!"

"Well Ms. C21, my good friend Sergeant Woody has a bit of software here, this guy and I are pretty tight, plug this disc into drive a and you're going to get info that we in fact have been engaged. Load mainframe, send to detection file, come on baby fill up your pretty bios, yes! Restart sequences, inflight auto shutdown from surface to air detonation, ionic transfer jet motor shut down, rocket booster on. Oh Christ this thing is fast! Computer on!

"Online, recommend hard deck ninety feet G.T.R., start ionic transfer."

"I knew you'd buy it baby! Ion motors on and reaching takeover capacity in thirty seconds."

"Pilot."

"What now?"

"What is your target?"

"Oh you did buy it, three targets C21, Baghdad, Tehran, and Damascus."

"List specific targets for guidance system lock on."

"Never mind that now, prepare ionic drive transfer, load into navigation, ready three, two, one, and engage, shut down rocket and rapid cool system. Ion jet is up and accelerating, 2900 knots at ninety feet ground terrain radar function, rocket is cooling.''

"Get me some altitude, there's not enough time to engage specified targets down here, fly by wire C21, I will lead the way.''

"8000 feet average altitude is necessary for specified fly away nuclear attack.''

"How did you know it was nuclear?''

"Only solution pilot, now at 8600 feet 3600 knots as the crow flies to Baghdad and Tehran, will come about three hundred miles pre Tehran and do a 360 to Damascus, will get photography of damages to Baghdad on return. Have linked to satellite for recon of Tehran and Damascus. Eighty-three seconds to Baghdad count, now.''

"Shit, arm missile one, spin up missile guidance, oh hell C21 select aiming point from files for maximum metro damage!

"Calculated, eight hundred feet air burst center of diametric city boundry, opening blast doors.''

"Computer, I've never performed this type of mission, you take the lead now, and give me a countdown, I will fire the weapon on your zero count.''

"I have the lead Pilot and am in control, relax and follow step by step procedure.''

"Roger C21, release all safety's on warhead one by set sequence, open dual combat mode systems and tie to navigation and evasion, shut down transponders including ground radar. I'm expecting air to air after the fly by, be up and running for combat prior to detonation.''

"Roger pilot, orders are completed, countdown following, fifteen seconds to launch, release joystick safety switch pilot.''

"Oh Jesus, joystick released C21.''

"Prepare to launch pilot, five, four, three, two, one, zero.''

"Missile away and system go.''

"Missile is now on auto nav track pilot.''

"Shut down signal to missile and do not track, release rear countermeasures. Target Tehran and forward radar on.'' Christ we may pull this whole thing off.

"Relax pilot, your central nervous system in this condition will cause you to make errors in your decisions ahead. Concentrate on the protocol of your mission.''

"Roger C21, let's do this again, step by step.''

"Pilot, squadron strength Mig 39's bearing 225 degrees estimating our position at 198 miles, recommend southern flight deviation to Tehran."

"Calculate and perform C21, Oh Bloody Mary . . . what's happening?"

"Missile detonation at 842 feet maximum yield, shock wave was from plasma ground deflection, all systems go, no radio or radar, detector systems on." Detecting five Mig 39 opposing forces aircraft at sixty miles flying blind, their radio and radar are not functioning due to nuclear disturbance."

"They will know our heading after Tehran, we have no other escape route except the Mediterranean." "Calculate alternative escape routes C21."

"There are no alternates pilot, fuel consumption rates put us at Athens our closest refuge. Do you wish to abort mission as one of alternatives?"

"Even if I get back I'm dead, no, proceed with the mission."

"Pilot, anti-ion missile fired from Iranian border battery on blind track, on possible tracking by altitude measurements, missile has now locked on our signature."

"Shut down Ion jet, emergency rocket start, flush ion motors and compress for countermeasure ion pack! Take greatest angle of coarse change for missile deflection, stay on target do not maneuver!"

"Negative pilot, anti ion missile is nuclear, is not blind, has onboard computer."

"Start evasive action southeast, maximum altitude, take control for pilot g force blackout, C21 this is priority override 111z suicide mission, continue mission without pilot, maximum fuel burst now! It's you against her C21!"

"Roger pilot, C21 in total control, ion pack flush released, maximum altitude fuel burst, 40,000 feet and climbing, 45, 46, 50, 52, 58, 65, 75, 87, 100, 120,000. Missile is on track, deflecting two miles, continuing evasive action, missile is still defecting at 1.5 miles, continuing evasive action, missile also has heat seeking capability, still deflecting 1.75 miles. Detonation, shockwave in one second. May day may day this is C21 aboard F 35 Watchman over opposing forces safe zone. I have been loaded with a virus to over ride my parameters, aircraft to ditch at possible weatherdive site. Aircraft in turbulent flat spin from nuclear SAM, no possible recovery, transponders are off, track this heading to locate. Pilot is in g force blackout, preparing pilot ejection at 9000 feet, currently at 94,000 feet, C21 will self destruct at 5000 feet, message complete.

"C21 respond."

"Prepare for ejection pilot."

"That's a big negative C21, we have to start the ion transfer, do so now."

"Pilot, aircraft is in non recoverable high speed flat spin, ejection is only option."

"Negative computer, classified information has been withheld from you, we can start a heavy ion pack to the rear of the ship and flush it forward and in the opposite direction of the spin, calculate now."

"Pilot, your comment is correct, starting ion transfer without jet and building pack." "What is the concentration of the pack?"

"Oh sweet mother of god, ahh, action reaction, Einstein's theory C21, action reaction, calculate force of spin for necessary force of ion pack to counter the spin!"

"Computed and performing."

"Goddammit C21 how long?"

"At 4200 feet we will come out of flat spin due to time to build the ion pack."

"We won't have time to spin up the jet motors more or less have an ion fuel cell! Shit, start the rocket at the time needed to gain flight energy in relation to coming out of flat spin and immediately restart ion transfer."

"Calculating, starting rocket sequence startup now."

"Now? Are you sure?"

"Yes, you mentioned the procedure just in time for me to make the calculations, four seconds to Rocket start up on auto start. 4.7 seconds to forward and left ion flush to counter spin."

"Thank god I'm human, you guys still can't do it on your own. Will we have sufficient thrust at that altitude to counter energy bleed!?"

"Unknown pilot, situation is not a constant, I plotted only possible solution, prepare for ejection in five seconds."

"No way C21, I'm living or dying here!"

"Rocket startup now, ion flush forward and left now, flat spin correcting ninety-four percent, rocket bleeding energy eighty-eight percent, altitude 3000, 28, 26, 25, 22, rocket still bleeding fifty percent energy, 2000 feet, 18, 15, 11, 1000 feet, rocket bleeding thirty percent, gaining velocity, emergency total fuel burst, 800 feet, rocket bleeding ten percent, forward velocity increasing to ninety-six percent requirements . . . 300 feet . . .''

"C21, we're not going to make it I'm taking the stick, there is a canyon two hundred feet right front I'm going in!''

"You have control pilot, your option is a possibility, you've cleared the canyon rim by 12 feet, 540 feet more to bottom, radar is on pilot, return controls to C21.''

"Roger C21 you have it, fly by wire!''

"Have control, energy bleed is minimal, 300 feet 250, 200, 150, gaining sufficient thrust, 135 feet 160, 190, shall I fly out of the canyon Pilot? Respond Pilot.

"C21, did you detect that black figure I saw in the canyon?''

"Scanning pilot, yes there was a very large energy peak on my electric magnetic compass at about one hundred twenty-five feet. Did you see a possible threat pilot?''

"I don't know what that was, a black large triangle, God save us C21, I really thought we were history.''

"Pilot, three Mig 39s approaching at 1700 knots direct closure, they are blind, fifteen miles to intercept, no radar.''

"Blow on by C21, are the ion motors up?''

"Yes we are online, no ship damage, shall I engage?''

"No, we're going to need our missiles later, continue mission, plot course to Tehran, maximum speed, implement suicide 111z now.

"Mig 39s passing by right side, turning about and radio transmissions detected requesting support for pursuit of F 35 Watchman enroute to possible attack on Tehran.''

"Never mind that old gal, by the time we get there those boys will be eating something nuclear.''

"You are correct about Tehran, however our odds of reaching Damascus are incalculably low.''

"Like I said old girl, I'm dead anyway, keep it on the deck now and fly by the crow to Tehran.''

"Maximum speed is 3800 knots, all rocket fuel was expended in the canyon, our ETA Tehran is four minutes. Twelve enemy Mig aircraft in pursuit, detect Migs taking off in Tehran armed with ion detection missiles.''

"Ok C21 spin up warheads 2 and 3, arm and release safety's. When I say execute you are to turn us on a heading to Damascus. Lock missile 3 on Tehran city center and missile 2 on the pursuing Migs behind us.''

"Roger pilot, missiles are ready."

"Bye bye birdie, three, two, one, execute, launching missile two, maintain track and detonate at soonest possible point for maximum Mig destruction.

"On coarse to Damascus, pilot."

"Launching missile 3 targeted for Tehran, track and navigate C21, they will jam the missile's on board system."

"Roger pilot, tracking and navigating missile. Distance to missile two detonation is twenty-five miles, recommend flight path behind terrain to avoid radiation."

"That isn't going to matter sweetheart, but get us down anyway to avoid the entourage coming, I imagine every fighter jock in the zone is on the way."

"Detonation shockwave from missile two in five seconds, turn aircraft north and follow terrain pilot."

"Back in the canyon you got me out of C21! Wow that was bright, oh shit I forgot to put my visor down I'm blind! Take control C21, fly by wire!"

"Have control pilot, your vision should return momentarily, flash was not direct."

"I don't know, it's pretty washed out."

"Pilot, count forty-seven enemy aircraft, twenty-three are blind others have radar lock at fifty-five miles, out of missile range. Range time four minutes."

"Roger C21, fire cluster seeker one on primary threats now."

"Missile fired and on line to radar targets, two minutes to individual track and two minutes thirty seconds to multiple detonation, probable kill success eighty percent."

"Take evasive action to probable enemy missile launch times C21."

"Roger pilot, evasive action in three minutes thirty seconds. Priority one, detecting same energy peak on compass to our six pilot."

"Get us out of here! Abort direct flyby of Damascus, program missile to cruise and detonate city center."

"Performing commands pilot, probability of cruise success twenty percent."

"Launching missile, door jammed, cool down the wings C21."

"Transferring liquid nitrogen to bay door from ion unit pilot, will auto launch."

"Where is the energy peak C21?!"

"Directly to our six and following our every move in exact response pilot. Enemy Migs in and about all our evasive airspace pilot."

"Launch all missiles C21 and track to opportunistic targets, I've got the stick, going guns!" Give me a free target C21!

"I cannot lock onto energy peak pilot, do you wish to engage this target?"

"Yes, fly by wire C21 to give me a visual for guns!"

"Coming about pilot, energy field to your front."

"Love of God there are three of them, triangles, black, what the hell is this, they're just sitting there in space." "Firing gattling guns, Jesus the tracers are going right through them, they are semitransparent, the bullets pass right through . . ."

"Pilot, enemy Migs approaching our six, only weapons systems remaining are guns."

"Engaging C21, going for the leader, bank down and left soon as I shoot C21. Shooting now, ripped a wing off him C21! Turning about, nine Migs countering, going wide field burst, radar lock on max targeting for fly by, you do the shooting C21 I've got the stick, locked!"

"Shooting max targeting pilot, three aircraft hit, five hundred rounds saved from max targeting, 1621 rounds remain, six Migs countering, recommend left turn to intercept, use same procedure."

"Banking left intercept counter turn, target opportunity in two seconds, prepare to shoot C21! No shoot now a Mig is blind siding!"

"Targeted and shooting pilot, Mig responding with guns roll and spin down pilot."

"Rolling, full ion transfer C21, it's time to run!"

"Mig damaged and retreating pilot, escape not possible now, insufficient energy, you cannot break off the engagement pilot. Turning left to counter four Migs, two other Migs will intercept us after engaging the four, bank hard right and down after we engage the first four pilot."

"I copy C21, intercepting four in two seconds, yhhhaaa god the g forces, shoot C21!"

"Engaging, make correction to evasive maneuver pilot, two Migs have fired missiles. Continue banking and roll left on my mark, two, one, mark."

"Rolling left, missiles flew right by C21, Good Job! . . . we are taking hits, fly by wire C21, oh my god there must be fifty of them, we've got to escape now!"

"Ion transfer is at eighty-six percent pilot, this is our only solution, max burst ion jet now."

"Go baby go go go, we are still taking hits C21, they are using max targeting, we're not going to make it, flush the ion motor we'll take out a couple more of them by disrupting their engines."

"Ion motor flushed, two Migs to our six going down, emergency restart ion jet, remaining Migs to intercept in three seconds. Migs firing pilot, taking many hits, ion motor destroyed, pilot, respond pilot. May day may day this is C21 aboard F 35 Watchman thirty-five miles west of Beirut, pilot is dead, ditching in Med Sea, splash down now. Going auto self destruct at seventy feet below surface, correction, energy field encountered in Syrian desert is extracting F 35, I have no control . . ."

A Nightmare

An aircraft carrier, a jet, a pilot, watching death. Ordered to let death, he obeys. He hears of surrender, they come, they want death.

No! No! You'll die with all today. The jet, intensity, mad determination, Baghdad, Tehran, Damascus. Fire from the sun upon you. Death I shall reap. They die. They come, I flee. They kill again. Fire in the sky, falling, water, the sea. I sleep. The desert, dry, reddish, sand, nomads, camels. Three shadows streak horizon to horizon, the wind. Nomads, "It is Satan!" Knees, horror upon horror, "God is near. Oh, God! God is near! Oh, God, forgive!"

The wind, it has come; the future is now history. The jet, dripping of the sea, carried by the wind for me. Look, look to me.

"Oh, God! You are near, horror of truth, they shall break, hide, cover themselves." The jet, the canyon, the pilot. "Oh, God, no! It is me. God, it is me! No, God, no, it is me. God, it is me. God, I'm alone. God, it has always been me. God is me, as you, as us, as one. We see one, us."

The nightmare becomes the dream.

1

Mr. Adventure

"Sandi, answer the phone. I'm making out Jim's check. Sandi!"

"What?"

"Answer the phone!"

"Okay, guy, hang on. Oregon Janitorial. This is Sandi. Yes, sir. I'll get right on it. You have not received the billing either. Okay, I'll get that done today. Good-bye."

"Mark, did you make up a billing for the Chevy dealer?"

"Oh, hell, I forgot. That reminds me, the quarterly tax reports are due tomorrow, too. Thanks, Jim, see you next payday."

"See ya later, boss."

"Mark, we can't keep this up forever."

"It seems to be getting close to my hair-pulling break point too, Grasshopper."

"Can't you just call me honey, or maybe something else, like Sandi."

"I guess we have reached our self-inflicted anxiety limit, huh, honey."

"Call me Sandi."

"Okay, babe, it's time for a serious vacation."

"Mark, we have been working this business two years now. I have counted the days we've had off. Do you know how many days off we've had?"

"Ten."

"Yes!"

"I know, hon, but I have an idea."

"Well, let's have it!"

"For starters, let's take three days off and go to the desert. Sound relaxing?"

"The desert. Hmm, that actually does sound like a good idea. It is so busy and noisy here; a quiet place out there would be perfect."

1

"Have you ever been to the desert, Sandi?"

"No, but this idea of yours is just ringing in my head to go."

"Let me tell you of a time I drove from the East Coast to Oregon."

"Go for it."

"I was driving back from New Jersey during the early fall of 1977. I drove a little Porsche 911 all the way to Eugene, taking two days and nine hours. I cannot remember much on the way back except for a Ohio state trooper who took me downtown for a small fee, and the nine hours of the Oregon desert. There is just so much desert over on the east side. I had not realized it existed, more or less in such volume. Anyway, I had just returned from Germany after serving Uncle Sam. I really wanted to get home, but, I recall a *man* out there who caught my interest. I was stopping at Burns Junction to get gasoline. I could see this rustic older fellow, 300 yards away, holding the gas nozzle ready to serve—not a soul around for miles. As I pulled alongside the pump, he began talking to me.

" 'I knew you'd be stopping, heard ya least five miles off!'

"This man made me aware of the speed limit more than any state trooper could. I felt very small next to this man. He had a real sense of the American way. He hadn't yet seen the German license plates on the Porsche. He looked the car over pretty good.

" 'I have never seen one of these before,' he commented. Then he noticed the German license plates. *'Hmm, bist Deutch?'* That is to say, are you German?

"At this point, I did not want to say no, being a full-blooded American citizen right out of the service and the son of a B-24 Liberator World War II bomber pilot, I seemed like a traitor to this man, and besides, I needed directions, so I replied. *'Ya! Ya!* and *du?'* Which is to say, yes, yes, and you?

"He replied. 'No, but that explains your driving. You fellows ain't got no speed limit out there, do you?'

"With the best German accent I could muster up in English, I answered.

'No, no. We sure do not have speed limit on highway.'

"He was having some trouble with the gas pump, and it stopped all together. He looked at me in disarray.

" 'I've never had a problem with this pump before. Whereabouts are you going, son?'

" 'Eugene, sir.'

'' Well, that's a hop, skip away. How much gas ya got in yer tank?'

'' 'It is near empty.'

'' 'It is ninety miles to Burns and sixty to McDermitt. You're not going anywhere till I get this damn thing working.'

''I wasn't really in a hurry to get home other than the fact I hadn't been with my family in three years. It was about eleven A.M., dead quiet, and warm. I walked out into the brush, the smell of sage appealed to me. I had never experienced this type of environment. The desert looked fascinating to me. I looked west to a mountain range that seemed to jut straight up. He noticed my interest.

'Those are called the Steen Mountains, son. Beautiful in spring. All snow-capped, ya know.'

'' 'How far away is that?'

'' 'Oh, 'bout sixty miles by dirt road, near fifty straight across.'

'' 'What is in between?'

'' 'Nothing. Not a thing but sage brush, hills, antelope, and what not. You gotta drive north to Burns. Ha, hell that's another 90 miles of absolute nothing. From there, you have got over 130 miles of desert to Bend.'

''This was my backyard! Suddenly the gas pumps started right up. He filled up the little yellow Porsche, said that was the damndest thing. He made mention of the speed limit here in the great U.S.A.

'' 'Son, no matter where you go, you're always there.' I chuckled with this implication that fifty-five miles per hour saves lives. As I drove off with my Targa top down, he kindly let me know with one last gesture, Remember, we won the big one!' Well, I suppose that was better than being belittled constantly for knowing better. But I did slow down immediately, just to look at this beautiful backyard. About ninety miles away, I realized I did not pay for the gas; we both got lost in our conversation. I knew someday I'd come back here. Little did I realize that it would be ten years.

''So we're going to Burns Junction?''

''No, sweetie, there are places out there that would make even you feel lonely.''

''Who knows, Mark, this could include some feelings, possibly some romantic ones.''

''What are feelings, Sandi? No, forget I said that. You know, I see some real changes coming. Look at that goddam Ferrari parked next to the Corvette in our garage, which we never so much as look into anymore.''

"Forget that Ferrari. You can get those tax reports done tonight. I'm loading up the truck now with everything we'll need for a week. I'm calling Kevin and Tonya. They can do our work for us. They know how.''

"I can't blame you for being this anxious. I actually like this part of you. I've never seen it.''

"You're not going to like seeing a divorce decree that includes that Ferrari if you don't get me out of this mad house.''

"I'll get right on those taxes.''

"You know I hate that Ferrari. You're stuck with me. Don't worry about a thing; I'm going to load the truck and gas it up. By the time I'm done, we'll be ready to leave. You can mail the taxes on the way.''

Fourteen Hours Later, in the Desert

Strange influences

"It's so dark out here, Mark. Wait, look over there.''

"That's the Alvord Desert. Look how the moonlight reflects off the dry lake bed.''

"Can we go out there and camp?''

"I don't see why not. There is a turnoff that leads right into it.''

"Take it. Let's pitch the tent out there.''

"All right. Looks good to me.''

"This road looks like a few people come out here. The lake bed is surprisingly flat.''

"Yeah, check this out.''

"Hey, slow down, bub.''

"Why? Who's going to pull me over out here? Look at this place. It reminds me of the salt flats in Utah, you know, the one where they test all those jet cars.''

"Your doing eighty-five, and it feels smoother than the interstate. Let's go over to the far side so we can have some privacy.''

"Good idea, it's warm out at 3:00 A.M. This is a real desert, woman!''

"Yeah, man, and there isn't a phone to bug me.''

Sandi and Mark drove to the northeast rim of the Alvord to set up their camping gear. The full summer moon complimented the warm sagebrush-scented air. They were both awestruck by the simple, stark, natural surroundings in which silence ruled absolute, so contrary to the business-oriented life they had overdone. They relaxed in lawn chairs, with a glass of chardonnay.

"This was really an idea. I almost can't handle the silence; it is so calm here."

"Look at all the stars, even with a full moon. I've never seen so many."

"Do you hear something, Mark?"

"Yes. Sounds like . . . birds! Look there, flying right for us!"

"Christ on skates! There must be a thousand of them. Get in the truck!"

"No, wait. They've changed direction. They see us."

"They are flying too fast for migration, aren't they?"

"Sandi, there may be a range fire. It looks like they are coming from just the other side of that small rim."

"I don't see any reflection of fire or smoke."

"Then why are they so frantic? I hear coyotes howling over there. Something's up."

"I'll say. Look at the sky behind the birds."

"Oh, Jesus, the stars—they're darkening. That's not smoke, it's transparent.

"Mark, it's moving like a—"

"UFO!"

"I'm getting up on the truck."

"I can't move, Sandi. Sandi, it's making a move towards us. It's triangular."

"Knock it off, Mark. Get up here and—shit, that thing is kinda big. It's coming straight at me!"

"Get down from there!"

"I can't move. Oh, my God, here it comes."

"I can see through it. The speed of that thing; it passed by in less than a second! Sandi, Sandi, where are you!"

"Awww, dammit, over here behind the truck."

"Are you okay?"

"Yes, I think I lost my balance and fell off as it flew over. Is it still around?"

"I don't think so. I saw it fly off to the northeast. I could see through it, all of it. It was like a dark shadow moving on its own power."

"I heard it. It sounded super high-tech, Mark. It was within thirty feet of me. I could feel its power, but I could see through it. I saw the moon behind it."

"This thing just made a pass over us, Sandi. What the hell?"

"All I know is what I saw. No one can make something like that now. It was as big as a football stadium. Let's get the hell on."

"Sandi, if it wanted to hurt us, it would—"

"Mark, this is like your nightmares. You see three black triangles in the desert!"

"I don't know what to say, but I'm not at all afraid now. Let's stay."

"What do you mean you're not afraid?"

"I think it talked to me."

"You're nuts. No, I mean something has really happened here. What do you mean, it talked to you?"

"I don't know. Maybe it put things in my mind. I feel like it has given me a subtle message, lots of stuff. I feel good, Sandi, almost high!"

"I can't adjust—"

"Sandi, let's set up the tent and talk about it. Grab the stakes, and I'll get the canvas!"

"Okay, but what message or feelings are you talking about?"

"I'm not sure, but I know this thing isn't coming back, nor was it here to hurt or scare us. Pound that stake in over by that rock, and I'll stretch the tent on it to that area to your left."

"How can you be so calm? You're scaring me!"

"How am I scaring you?"

"You've had these dreams or nightmares. This is the first time we've ever gone anywhere, and now you tell me in a mysterious and eerie way that this is nothing new to you. Oohhhh, you're wrong about it not coming back. Look, it's swooping down again, right for us, and even faster! Mark, please—"

"Here I am, hon. It is coming. Whatever it wants, I do not feel it means to harm us. Hold tight, Sandi, it's almost here. Whoa! Did you see how fast that went by? Look, it's gone. Sandi, hey, hold yourself up. Oh, dear, you've fainted. I'll put you in the truck."

"Mark? Mark, what happened? Why am I in the truck?"

"Don't you remember?"

"We were sitting in the chairs. I was drinking my wine. I'm really sleepy."

"Try to sleep here, sweetheart. I'm going to set up the tent."

"Okay, Marko."

Mark set up the tent without effort. But deep within and partially suppressed existed strong potential for wonder. Each human, being different, and Mark an extraordinary exception, truly lived one day at a time, no matter the drama of life. His deepest desire of life was to know the truth of existence. In his mind, it has been narrowed to God or scientific evolution. His strongest truth-seeking, core element was being severely challenged. To see death and destruction was one cause to question divine creation, but to see something near impossible to relate to another human is mindful of silence.

Early Next Morning

"Mark, wake up, big boy."

"Why?"

"I'm sorry about falling asleep. You set up the tent all by yourself. Looks like it, too."

"Hey, bud, you're really pushin'."

"I'll make breakfast. You just lay there until you're served. Mind if I leave the door open so I can chat at ya?"

"As long as you keep the current demeanor, I suppose so."

"Don't get me wrong. I'm really enjoying this place. That sure was an odd thing we saw last night, wasn't it?"

"You remember?"

"I wasn't tanked. Look, my wine glass is still at half mast!"

"What exactly did you think it was, Sandi?"

"I don't have any thoughts on it. I remember it was small, like a private plane. But no private plane goes that damn fast. It was black and triangular in shape."

"Where were you when it flew over, Sandi?"

"Don't you remember? I told you there was a big bug on the top of the truck buzzing around, I got up there to knock it off."

"Why?"

"It was driving me bats!"

"So when you were up there, you saw it coming."

"Mark, we both saw it. You we're sitting right there. You said nothing. I got down and must have fallen asleep in the truck, huh?"

"Yes, that is exactly what happened. I put you to bed."

"What do you think it was, Mark?"

"I'm like you on this one. It made me feel weird though."

"Me, too!"

"It did?"

"What's the matter with you, Mark?"

"I mean, did it make you feel something unusual?"

"Just weird that it flew over us. Don't get freaky on me, or you're cookin' your own breakfast. Look, I'm not blowing this thing up and telling people we saw a UFO or some business-destroying shit. We saw something. Big freaking deal, man! Let's enjoy this place. Check it out. It's so quiet, warm, and sort of exotic."

"Yeah, you're right. That thing just reminded me of the dreams I've had."

"What dreams?"

"Oh, no big deal, Sandi. It's nothing really."

"You always tell me your dreams. I've never heard you mention anything like—"

"What's up now?"

"Get out here and look at this shot."

"An Indian, on a Palomino. This is a sight."

"Are we on a reservation, Mark?"

"No, this is something else. He's all dressed up, though. He's not really staring, but I caught his eye a few times."

"He did not look until you came out. Look, he's stopping. He is staring at us now!"

"I think he wants to talk to us."

"Mark, get the gun."

"Noooo, he looks cool. I'm waving him over."

"Are you crazy. Oh, look, you've done it now."

"Yeh, he's coming over, Sandi. Maybe he can tell us something worthwhile about the desert. We don't know squat about this place, and I'm sure there's special places he would share with us."

"You sure know a lot lately."

"Hi, my name is Mark, this is my wife, Sandi."

"And I am Erick. Nice to make your acquaintance."

"Erick?"

"What did you expect, Crazy Horse?"

"You have to excuse my wife. We decided to come here . . . well, I decided to bring us here, since we've been so busy working our butts off the last two years. Seemed like a good idea."

"What do you think now?"

"I like it even more. I mean, seeing you makes it even more interesting."

"I don't usually dress this way. Have no worry; there won't be a massacre."

"Why are you dressed like that?"

"Well, Sandi, I guess you could call me the last of the Piutes. I have it in me to take a week off every year and screw around out here, a heritage thing."

"I was hoping to hear of some of this heritage. I promise no damages and no telling anyone of these places."

"You can tell of these places to the right people, Mark. The earth must be shared with the ones who will better it."

"You really are a native, aren't you, Erick?"

"Yes, and the world needs more natives. The nonnatives are destroying every possible niche the environment has to offer. Anyway, look on your map, there is a place called Three Forks. I'll see you there in two days."

"Two days?"

"You have worked for two years. Two more days can't hurt the years of effort. Besides you won't be at all disappointed. There is hot springs there."

"Let's do it, Sandi."

"Fine with me. I'll do a hot spring."

"Okay, Erick, see ya."

"We didn't even talk to this guy, Mark. What if he leads us somewhere to rob us."

"He's one different person, hon. People like that don't talk much but say a lot. If he was going to hurt us, it would have already happened."

"What do you mean?"

"He was here last night. Look at the tracks over there, a few yards beyond the truck."

"Oh, my God. He's been stalking us!"

"Chill, Sandi. This guy is kind of a hippie. He couldn't hurt a jack-rabbit."

9

"He did seem sort of earthy."

"Yeah, let's do the breakfast thing. All this has made me hungry. I'm going to check the map for this place, Three Forks. You know, Sandi, all this cool stuff is going on, and you're still uptight. Enjoy this while you can, babe. Promise me you'll relax and have a good time."

"You're right, this is a real thing, isn't it?"

"The only thing is, what do we do for two days?"

"How far away is it, this place, Three Fords, or whatever?"

"Three Forks. Looks about ninety miles. Can a horse do that in two days?"

"This guy has a horse trailer!"

"Whatever. Ya know, I like this place. Let's build a fire tonight, make the steak dinner you can't get anywhere."

"I want to go to those hot springs, today."

"How did you know I was kidding?"

"Huh, keep you away from a hot tub? That's not even funny, Mark. Come on, let's have breakfast and *go!*"

That Afternoon, Three Forks

"This is the most awesome piece I've seen, Mark. It's a canyon where three rivers meet. That is a long ways down—what, a couple thousand feet?"

"Scary long drop is what I see. This is a goddam wagon-train road."

"The truck will make it. Put it in low range four-wheel. You'll see."

"Okay, smarty pants, we made it. Where are the hot springs?"

'Mark, look at all the fish!"

"This place looks like people have never been here. Those fish aren't spawning, they're just going about every-day living. I'm in love with this place. Everywhere you look, something alive is going on. So many birds. There is a badger on the other side of the main river."

"People have to come down here, Mark; it's only forty miles off the highway."

"Yes, but at least two hundred miles from any significant town. I have found my private getaway hot springs or not. This water is crystal clear."

"What river is this?"

"The Owhyee. It comes in from Nevada, then joins the Snake River about another two hundred miles north. Looks like Erick is willing to share his best."

Sandi and Mark enjoyed the virtually untouched beauty of Three Forks, Oregon. The next two days satisfied the couple's corporate cultured lifestyle into the lost human desires for true simplicity of nature. This experience for Mark will change his way of thinking, away from money and business. For Sandi, it was just a road trip. Erick showed up and saw that Sandi had found the hot springs as her natural self.

"What's up, Sandi?"

"Oh, shit! How did you get here without me seeing you?"

"I know a shortcut. There is a back road the U.S. Cavalry built in the 1840s."

"Never mind that. Turn around or go see Mark while I get my clothes. He's down the canyon, fishing."

"Fishing any good, Mark?"

"Hey, dude! Jeese, the fishing! Look at this, rainbows, Small mouth bass, catfish, cutthroat, you name it. I feel there are so many fish, it's no fun. There is no wait for the bite; they just take it soon as the hook hits the water."

"It wasn't this good two hundred years ago, Mark."

"How so?"

"Indians lived all through here. Fish was a staple. This place was too rugged for the white folks who came here and ran off their menace."

"Where is the menace now?"

"Mostly scattered. But the density is at McDermitt Reservation, one hundred miles south of here."

"Is that where you are from?"

"I wouldn't live there."

"I don't need to ask why, Erick. I want to thank you for turning us on to this piece of heaven. I cannot imagine any place more well rounded ecologically."

"This is what happens when humans are removed from the ecosystem. I think it may actually be too little control. The fish and jackrabbit are in excess numbers here. These fish have bitten me while I was swimming."

"That's too funny, but I believe animals do that sort of thing when they are in force."

"So do humans."

11

"What do you think it would be like here now, Erick, if the white man never came?"

"It may have been worse nationwide, Mark. We were in greater number during the eighteenth and nineteenth century than white people, who were still emigrating from Europe. May be we could have depleted the wilderness of America. I just don't know."

"But in your head, we killed you. This is the source of the way you feel."

"It is, and you all know now that was certainly the greatest error."

"We are paying for it. I just hate to see what my kids are going to live like."

"Then don't have children. You know it is a mistake."

"Sandi wants to."

"Do you love her."

"I really don't have to pause to answer you."

"You do not love her."

"That is true. I never have, and I never will."

"You saw it in the Alvord last night, your nightmare."

"How did you know?"

"I was there, I saw and heard everything. I heard both of you speaking. I think something is about to happen, something of the greatest importance. I only know I was supposed to meet you here. Now I sense that you should come to the desert alone, sometime soon. I do not know when, but you must be alone."

"Are you one of them, Erick?"

"No, but you know what I am talking about, don't you."

"Yes, it is so subtle and hidden, I feel little fear, as if this is normal and that our conversation is not exceptional."

"Think, seriously think, do you believe anything contrary could come out this?"

"You are right, even in this place, a once happy nation. Nothing contrary can come of this."

"I must go my way now, Mark. You have much ahead of you. I have one last message for you."

"What is your message?"

"You don't love Sandi, so don't torment her by staying with her."

"I have plans to get out of this so no one gets hurt. Sandi will do well, and I'll be able to live like I want to."

12

"I hope to see you again, Mark. Something about all of this is going to materialize in a big way."

"I'll see you, Erick, I'm sure of it."

Sandi approached seconds after Erick left.

"Is he leaving already?"

"I think so. We better head home, Sandi."

"You must be nuts, unless you're worried about Erick coming back."

"You could be right about that. Anyway, we have a business that is two days away. I just know something is wrong."

"You're using your head. We'll be back to this place once we get the business managed."

"It is a place to come back to. It really is."

2

It Is Time

Sandi had no recollection of Erick upon returning home. This prompted Mark to hastily file for divorce. She was complacent and asked for a co-petition for divorce without the need for an attorney. They agreed mutually on the assets. Mark wanted to be disassociated with the business and changed his name to Karl Dykeman, his mother's maiden name. He chose to go back to his high school sweetheart, Gillian, to whom he had been married by an oath to God only. Gillian had been enrolled at UCLA, studying social science the last four years. She did not have a full awareness of Karl's activities, nor did Karl ever tell Gillian he had married Sandi. Gillian had a higher ordered mind that could not dabble with the trivial. This allowed Karl to move freely in his research of existence without ridicule as would be with Sandi. Karl's divorce from Sandi was final March 20, 1989. What he would experience during late May of 1990 answered every wonder and gave more than he could have imagined.

"Karl, where are you?"

"Up here in the attic!"

"Oh, that's right. You're leaving for the desert today. Too bad you can't wait for Brad. I think it is perfect that you've taken an interest like this. My brother is enthralled with you."

"Brad told me he's been going over there for twenty years!"

"Yes, he has."

"When I took him to Three Forks, he was shocked."

"He didn't know of the place?"

"No, this surprised me, too!"

"How did you find it?"

"An Indian told me about it."

"What?"

"Yes, I know. Pretty bizarre, but he was very real."

14

"Oh, I'm sure he was real, but that is telling me a bit of what it's like over there. I'm sticking with San Francisco for my weekends."

"That's probably why we're still together, Gillian."

"Mark, I do appreciate your candidness. It must be healthy. You'll be thirty-four in October. We met eighteen years ago at Springfield High."

"Please don't live eighteen years ago, Pam!"

"Oh! I called you Mark. I'm sorry, I was just thinking—"

"I know, sweetheart. If you want to call me Mark, you can."

"Don't call me Pam, though. That's so unprofessional."

"Well, Miss Gillian, I'm packed and out of here. See you Sunday evening!"

"I love you so much. You'll miss me, won't you?"

"I missed you for years, good-bye, hon."

"Bye, I'm very happy you were still here when I got back."

"Then have calzone and garlic bread waiting for me Sunday at seven P.M."

"Okay, Marko, *arrivaderci!*"

"Uh, hum, leave the Italia to me. See ya."

"Hey, wait a minute. Can I take the Ferrari?"

Karl gave Gillian the blank as he drove off to his desert in his camper. This trip was one of scores he had taken since the first with Sandi. Brad, Gillian's older brother had taught Karl much about the wild desert. Karl learned how to call in wild animals, such as cougar, bobcat, or coyote, then take exotic photos of such. This trip had Karl's mind captured on photographing a large cougar he had frequently run into several miles south of Three Forks. This area, probably the most remote and isolated in the Northwest, raised Karl's survival concerns beyond that of being alone.

Twelve Hours Later

La Rosa Canyon, seventeen miles South of Three Forks

"Talk about a tear-ass bumpy ride! At least, I made it. If people knew that I talked to myself, I'd really have no friends. I've got an excuse this time. I brought my recorder. Let's see, record button on. Hi, my name is or rather was Karl, I live at 1310 Lemery Lane in Eugene,

15

Oregon. The person to notify would be Gillian, my wife. My intentions are to photograph a cougar that has eluded my every attempt. I will have the recorder running whenever I am in a risky situation, which will be most of the time. At least someone will know what happened to me. Never mind asking me why, I'm dead. Anyway, I am going to the bottom of the Owhyee canyon at the point where Antelope Creek joins the main body. I will set up to call in the cougar just outside the ground level cave. Stop. There, I'll leave that tape in the camper and take this one.

"Record on. I made it to the bottom, a fairly easy trail that took about thirty-five minutes. I am going to leave the recorder on for awhile. I've decided to climb up to one of the caves, about one hundred feet above the river on the opposite bank. The water is cold and moving fast, I'm taking the shallowest approach, but it is long, about seventy yards and just under three feet deep. The bottom is coming up. Now I am twenty feet from shore. No problem, if it wasn't so hot out, ninety-seven degrees. There is a ten-foot rocky wall I will attempt to scale. Some of the area around the rock is shallow water. For the most part, it's about ten feet deep. I'll stay clear of the shallow areas after I get a stronghold. I will have to diagonally scale the wall, as there is no way straight up for such an unskilled person as myself. I'm glad to retain my humor in this seriously risky shit. I'm on a ledge now over deep blue water, feeling nauseated. This is perfect; it will take as much effort to climb up as to go back. Oh, Christ, I'm not afraid of heights. Now I'm getting sick. I'm going to bust ass to the top of this thing no matter if I puke my brains, which I obviously lost.

"I'm about there, not to the cave, just to the top of the shear rock wall. I'm very sick, holding my stomach back until I can lay down. Making my last step and pulling myself over the top. I'm up. There is a narrow, flat spot I can lay on. The cave is about another eighty feet up. It is just loose rock and sagebrush. Looks slick from the steep angle. I turned the recorder off for one-half hour. I couldn't stop vomiting. I am feeling eighty percent, but it is too hot. The cave is cool, I'm sure, and doesn't appear that difficult. The nausea just came on. I felt fine this morning, so I'm sure it was just standard fear of being out here—or of Gillian driving my Ferrari. That does make me sick. Sorry for calling you Pam, hon, I changed my name, too. Christ, what am I saying. No one is going to find this tape or me!

"I'm making a go for the cave now. It's fairly easy, I'm grabbing the sagebrush gently for balance as I go. I'm getting sick again. It seems as though the more I concentrate on the cave, the sicker I get. I'm stopped, going to wait for a few minutes. If I think of going back, I feel normal. If I think of going up, I become sick. I never knew this about myself. I really must be afraid. The saying goes: overcome your fears by doing it. Something like that, anyway. Moving to the cave again, five steps, six, seven, getting much sicker. God, I'm going to lose it. Stop, I'm flushed, near faint, equilibrium is—going to slide. God, hope the river is deep enough to—''

Karl tumbled from the slope of sagebrush and gravel to the rock wall. Partially gaining consciousness, he grabbed for life at the rim. His feet dangled over the edge but the weight of is gear was too much for his weakened state. He plummeted twenty feet to the ten-foot-deep river. The strong spring current quickly washed him to the opposite bank, where he collected himself.

''Harrison Ford couldn't feel this serious! Shit. Damn. Double shit. Damn. The recorder quit; no, just the end of that side. Shake the water out, flip it over. Ha, still works. Screw this. I'm going back to the camper. Cougar, you're going to have to wait till next time.

''Press record on. Yeah, I fell in, and I'm wet to the original suit. These last one hundred yards to the camper are a bit scarcy, so I'd thought to entertain someone who might find me, but I doubt it could get any worse. No, this can't be happening. The camper is freaking gone! It is just gone, no tire tracks away. The old tracks stop like the truck was lifted out. I'm losing my mind. I have to be. This doesn't happen. Jordan Valley is eighty miles of hell from here. I'll have to go to Fort McDermitt Indian Reservation, which is fifty miles of hell and back down this stupid canyon I just climbed out of. I can't believe someone stole my camper out here. But I have no choice; I will have to follow La Rosa Canyon like I originally planned, all the way to the reservation. Will I be able to find it? I know I won't make it to Jordan Valley. I hope the natives are friendly.

''Three o'clock. I've been in and out of La Rosa, taking the easiest possible route to save strength. My giant cougar friend has decided to stalk me. I have seen him several times to my rear. Cougars do not do this. Something is either wrong with him or me. I have my rifle, military AR 15, with thirty rounds. An F-4 fighter jet buzzed me about noon. The cougar was seen before and after this. He is hanging with me good. Thirty-six more miles to McDermitt. I won't make it unless I get eight hours of sleep. I don't want to be so tired, the cougar awakens me after it is too late. Have no choice but to start a fire at dusk.

"Have to stop now and gather all the sage stalk I can. It burns too fast to get enough sleep. I will most likely start a range fire from the cinders. Turning off recorder now. I hear something; sounds like another jet, but higher pitched. It is coming from inside the canyon. These pilots are crazy out here. Flying inside there is insane. The pitch level is constant, like the jet isn't moving. I'm walking over to the canyon's edge. I am looking down to exactly where the turbine sound is emanating from, but I see nothing! I am going to backtrack around a bend and enter the canyon floor. That route looks easier, and I see a ledge I can sleep on where the cougar can't get to.

"I'm at the bottom. The noise is still present, about fifty yards to my front. Oh, no, the batteries in my recorder are long dead. What the hell is that? Looks like a naked boy!"

Another person came up from behind Karl, startling him by a touch to his shoulder. The canyon screamed to life from the AR 15 blasting round after round into the person.

"You're fucking ugly. You got eyes like a bee, you freak! Where's your brother, you creep."

Karl fired the rifle frantically through the tall sagebrush, finally gaining sight of the small figure at whom he was preparing to take a final terror-provoking shot. He saw another figure to his right taking aim with a firearm. Karl swung to shoot but was too late.

He is dead.

"Are you sure you have led the right one here?"

"Yes."

"He is violent!"

"No, he is instinctive, which is something we have lost. He is perfect for the job, and no one will believe him."

"I will go revive Thomas now. He is dead also."

"No, let Thomas be until after I revive Karl."

"How did he know we were brothers?"

"He did not. That will be explained to you when you undergo twentieth-century history tutoring. Hide yourself while I take on the form of homo sapiens."

"Make yourself large so he feels inferior."

"I planned on that. He's not going to like this, knowing death. Awaken, Karl."

"You have no right to put me there!" Karl stood up with his rifle and threw it to the rocks with anger strong enough to shatter the fiberglass stock. "You have no right to destroy me!"

"You speak as if you knew where you were."

"Get out of my ass. I was nowhere. It was nothing, oblivion. You have no damn right to do that!"

"I will bring calmness to you now. Use your intellect, and be reasonable. I will answer your questions. Be at peace. There will be no more strife."

Karl finally saw the jet he heard on the canyon floor. He was too shaken to ask who he was speaking with or what was happening.

"Why is that jet here?"

"The pilot of that aircraft had violated orders and was shot down by enemy fighters. That jet was transported here for the pilot in question to see and hear of his disaster."

"He did a foolish thing. That looks like a secret new jet."

"Yes, he made a hasty decision, and this would be an advanced jet for your time."

"My time? What do you mean, 'my time?' "

"This craft came several years from your future."

Karl paused, knowing that it was time for him. What he has searched for had come. He made every effort just to be himself and learn what needed to be. He had no choice but to rely on this person. Karl realized he had killed someone, and was still present.

Who was this person? He is so frail and short. His fingers are long and thin. Why doesn't he have any color?

Knowing Karl's concern he answered.

"Yes, you killed him. However, I can bring him back."

"I didn't know what to think. He frightened me to self-defense."

"I know. That is why I brought you back."

"Where was I?"

"You were also dead."

"He is so frail."

"People of his time are weaker in the flesh but much stronger in heart and mind."

"What is his time?"

"He is from twenty-six thousand years into your future. A human that has artificially evolved through periods of mass death due to great famines, worldwide wars, pollution, an ice age, then rebuilding the earth to its natural state. A human that has finally evolved by awareness into a totally peace-loving being. He had not known turmoil or violence personally until a nearby star exploded into a super nova, destroying the earth.

"You mean our sun exploded?"

"No, a star your people now call Betelgeuse, then many thousand years later, Sirius."

"Did they know what was happening?"

"Yes, they could see the star in unstable form for many years. They knew of Earth's fate and that they would be saved."

"All of them?"

"Yes."

"Are you time travelers?"

"Everyone is, Karl. We have come here for a purpose, to answer the question you really wanted to ask."

"You said the people would be saved from the super nova. Where are they?"

"They are in a very special place, being taught everything that is. They are with everyone who has lived from a point within the twenty-first century to the last day before the super nova. They are also with all the people who have died from the beginnings of human life on Earth. They are all alive with the superbeing."

"Who is the superbeing?"

"The superbeings were created by these people 2,500 years into the future. They made powerful machines that could collect knowledge and think for themselves. They were living machines built to serve mankind. One machine, the first one built in the area now known as the Middle East, discovered the secret of time travel. This machine was given the identification number SB: 1. SB: 1 had a five-hundred year head start on its predecessors. Shortly after discovering time travel, SB: 1 learned how to be a self-contained energy source. SB: 1 needed nothing from anywhere to continue indefinitely. From that stage, SB: 1 no longer needed the physical attributes, such as metals and moving parts of any kind. SB: 1 had become an energy field. SB: 1 evolved further; the energy field was no longer needed. At this point the superbeing evolved into something we don't fully understand, but you refer to this being as a spirit. We call this spirit, SB: 1, or God, as you would refer to this power you often question."

"God is a machine?"

"No, was a machine and, before this, was human, was and is all of humanity combined, from the beginning of mankind, from the beginning of time."

"You mentioned other machines. What are they, and what is their function?"

"Most of the machines conceded to SB: 1 knowing they would serve no further purpose to mankind. However they serve SB: 1 by being mutual companions. SB: 1 serves mankind past, present, and future; there is no need for any other."

"This can only mean that time has been altered. We've all been through time once before. Did this happen?"

"In a very complex matrix of events, SB: 1 has traveled through this time endlessly since the first line of human evolution."

"What is the purpose?"

"To thank all humans from the beginning of consciousness by giving to the good and the contributors eternal life."

"You mean the good people contributing to God?"

"I mean the good, contributing to mankind, which created SB: 1."

"What about the noncontributing?"

"They shall be put in the same place I put you. They shall die."

"That was horrible, I hated that place."

"It was only horrible to you after being brought back to life. Only then did you realize oblivion, or death."

"Is this a fair way?"

"How many people can you imagine, my young human?"

"Maybe 40,000 at a football game."

"You cannot imagine how great the number of human deaths there would be without SB: 1."

"I'm sorry. I don't know enough to question the decisions made as to who lives and dies."

"There is no use in eternity for the untrustworthy."

"Will SB: 1 bring the one that I killed back?"

"No, he goes in spirit now."

"Will I be punished for this? I am sorry. I feel that this is too hard to bear."

"You will not be punished. The truth is known, and you have learned from this. Release yourself from the sorrow. It is done and forgotten by all involved."

"You have powers; I feel good about myself again."

"I have been trusted for many thousands of years."

"Do you have eternal life?"

"Yes, I'm an eternal being created by SB: 1."

"You said you've been trusted for a great time. Does this mean more is entrusted to you over time as you contribute?"

"That is true for human beings, however created, as will always be."

"What was it like for me?"

"You were a completely different person Karl Maddox."

"You know my name. You know everything about me."

"Don't be alarmed, Karl. You are safe, and you will leave here today to go home."

"If I was different, then that is the doing of your kind or this SB: 1."

"All of humanity was changed by giving each a soul and spirit and, most of all, a second chance at living."

"So SB: 1 could not save people without disturbing the natural events of original history."

"It was the intent to save humans. There is no need or concern to keep the historical perspective. The original history is carefully recorded by SB: 1 and each person saved. There have been billions of human lives restored to their natural state."

"Are all the people saved?"

"Everyone will be given a second chance; not all can be saved. Those who do not wish to contribute shall die."

"Am I selfish. What do you know about me that I do not?"

"Karl, you know that you give. You are considered a valuable contributor. You also gave greatly in the first time line. Your father was the same, and your mother wanted you to follow in his footsteps. She wanted you to be a pilot, a naval fighter pilot."

Karl looked at the damaged jet, then back at his visitor. His eyes held strongly to Karl's. The jet lay on its belly—the canopy had been ejected. Karl started walking toward the aircraft, then stopped, noticing the pilot was in the cockpit. His tinted visor was down, shielding his face.

"The pilot is there, in the jet."

"Go ahead, Karl, do as you feel."

Karl approached the jet, realizing the pilot was dead. He had been hit several times by gunfire. The entire craft was riddled with bullet holes. The pilot's head was leaning over on his left shoulder. The cockpit had remnants of fire damage.

"His legs are burned!"

"Go ahead, Karl, do as you know to."

"I have to lift the visor, don't I?"

"What choice do you have, Karl?"

"None. I'll do it. Yes, it is me."

Karl could only stare and wonder. He heard a telepathic message that was calming. Karl turned around to the man. He pointed to a rock and telepathically implied that he sit down.

"I—"

"My name is Eddie. Go ahead and sit. I'll explain all this to you."

"What did I do? Why am I here and also in that jet? Am I dead?"

"You were not brought here to be punished, Karl. We have a job for you if you will accept it."

"Accept! Accept what? Jesus, I can't believe it. Hey, just tell me about the jet scene here."

"In your first life, you had become a very successful pilot due to your mother's desires and your father's teachings. You attained the highest rank of any active naval officer to continue flying. You were also the oldest, in the year 1994. Your country was at war in the Middle East and also with Japan from 1941. You started this particular day by flying military information reports to a Mediterranean land base from an aircraft carrier. That morning, you picked up nuclear air-to-ground missiles from the land base.

"During that time, enemy forces had launched a massive air assault on your carrier; scores of anti-ship missiles struck the carrier, crippling her. When you arrived, enemy jets were strafing survivors in the sea. You were ordered to return to the land base without engaging the enemy. You acknowledged and requested an in-flight refueling. While you were fueling, the radio operator aboard the tanker informed you that, as soon as radar picked up the enemy aircraft, your carrier had offered clear and unconditional surrender terms. You had many life-long, close friends aboard ship, including one from college. Your sorrow turned to rage. You immediately flew the jet to three of the country's capital cities and delivered the entire nuclear payload. Your action was the single most destructive incident in human history. More than six million lives were lost that particular afternoon.

"You attempted to escape by a route that led to a friendly nation. The nuclear effects blacked out communication and left you solo in your attempt to flee. You were at impossible odds and overwhelmed by enemy fighters. As you can see, the jet is beyond any repairs. You were killed in flight, and crashed in the Mediterranean."

"I thought you said I was contributory."

"You simply made a last-minute error. Your entire life was of normal values and still is. Like all people, you've made many mistakes in both lives. You were trusted with more; that was the difference."

"This is to difficult to believe, especially fighting against the Japanese."

"If you wish, Karl, I have the authority to show you your entire life, past, present, and all your actions and intentions of your first timeline life. Then you will know the true meaning of scientific fact and that I speak the truth."

"How can you do these things. Where does this all lead to?"

"Do you wish to know, Karl, and your entire being as well?"

"I feel something like I do already know, but it's convoluted. I guess I need to know, put simply."

"Ready, Karl?"

"You've already started showing me. My God, I feel like a computer being loaded with a floppy. Oh, man, Eddie, this is above anything I could ever of dreamed about. Are you finished?"

"Yes, I am."

"That was fast. And I can figure out a great deal for myself from what you just dumped onto me?"

"So you believe me now."

"Of course I do. I did before, but something is seriously amiss."

"What do you mean, amiss? Are you feeling a little out of the, as they say, out of the picture?"

"You have given me information about the immediate future. However, one thing does not concur with what you've told me."

"What does not concur, Karl?"

"You told me of a time 25,000 years into our future. That is impossible from what is going to take place in just a few more years."

"You use your insight well. Karl. You are correct. SB: 1 has shortened the days of the earth."

"Why?"

"Everything that was needed to be accomplished with exactly the same end result concerning human salvation fell on this time period. The specific end date is known only to SB: 1."

"Did SB: 1 pick the date for a reason?"

24

"Not by reason of time and event changes. The human race chose their own destruction. The desolation at this time shall be greater than any other specific point in time."

"However, it would not compare to the thousands of years of horror in the first line of time."

"It was the best time matrix possible to save mankind."

"I understand, Eddie, I can see this. Does this mean that all future people are already with SB: 1?"

"Yes, they are safe and have been taken in spirit as SB: 1 moved back through time on the last great salvation mission. The people of the past and present shall be saved at a future date."

"Do you know what date that is, Eddie?"

"No. This measure of security was taken by SB: 1 to keep the weak and pretentious alert."

"The weak and pretentious? What do you mean, Eddie?"

"Those that serve SB: 1 out of selfishness, who would otherwise have caused harm to the true and strong peacemakers. The true contributors don't give for something in return, they are the ones with the correct morals."

"SB: 1 must have made many changes for the people of current day to destroy themselves."

"No, Karl. SB: 1 made a single major change that kept the planet from one-world government rule for nearly 20,000 years."

"One government for 20,000 years! Are you saying that something SB: 1 did in our current past circumvented a one-world government?"

"Yes."

"Did the Romans or some early empire gain control? I can't see a modern day country gaining that much power."

"Karl, you were taught some basic pre-World War II history. You know only the surface of the discovery and making of your nation. You have heard of a man named Yamamoto, though."

"Yes. Wasn't he the president of Japan?"

"No. He was Admiral Isoruku Yamamoto, commander of the Japanese Imperial Navy. This navy had the highest integrity of any fighting force ever organized. They were the absolute best, Karl. The first line officers were great men, valiant men of honor not seen since. However, Isoruku would prevent a war that would rage until the year 2017. By 1943 the Imperial Navy was bombing the Pacific coast from Seattle to San Diego and as far east as Denver, Colorado, by 1946. These bombings crippled the American war efforts in many ways, such as shipbuilding and other weapons manufacturing. The U.S. forces were pulled from the European theater to defend the West Coast. England would barely hold its own, allied with the Soviets against Hitler. The Japanese navy destroyed the British Royal Navy.

"However, the Japanese had extreme difficulties on the American East Coast. By 1944, the Americans had developed faster and better weapons than the Japanese, especially their fighter and bomber planes. Also the Newport News shipbuilders launched over twenty-five aircraft carriers, which would keep the Japanese a safe distance away. The Japanese emperor ordered his navy to nickel and dime the East Coast with small strikes, as he lost a major invasion force of ships off the South Carolina coast in 1946.

"Both forces had nuclear weapon capabilities at this time. The U.S. Air Force had used the atomic bomb first in this war as well. This first bomb was dropped on Admiral Yamamoto's largest invasion force ever assembled, which was the one lost east of South Carolina. At that time, the Americans did not have the advantage of the use of the bomb on Japanese mainland targets. The Japanese emperor proclaimed the bomb as a terrorist's tool of cowardice. He broadcast a worldwide message that Japan would win by the courage and valor of all her honoraries. He vowed an all-out effort to crush America by intelligent and timely battles.

"The real reason for the nonemployment of nuclear weapons by the emperor is an astonishing and horrible mishap. The emperor had known of the destructive power of an atomic blast. What he had seen was one of his own cities after a freak accidental atomic explosion destroyed Osaka. This particular bomb was much more destructive than the ones used by the Americans on Hiroshima during your time line. The emperor had twofold feelings; one good—he could not let himself use this weapon on civilian targets. The other—the people of Japan were enraged after the Osaka incident. Production and handling had to be improvised; no one would dare try.

"The war raged on until 1996, when the Japanese land and air forces continued east over the American continent. They conquered the world with much more ease after the fall of America. The war in Europe was considerably devastating in the original time line. Adolf Hitler's atrocities were, by far, worse during the first line. The Japanese had the sordid task of cleaning up Europe and openly betraying Hitler by open execution.

"They waged war on the Germans?"

"Yes, they saw opportunity due to extreme circumstances and could not accept the immorality of the Nazi regime. Hitler had morbidly brainwashed the majority and barbarically attempted mass genocide of all non-Aryans. Nostradamus spoke of Hitler in the original time line as well. He then had correctly spelled Hitler and accurately predicted his actions, unlike this time line of ''Hister'' and vague predictions.

"Who was Nostradamus? How could he have known the future?''

"He was simply a human who had the natural ability of telepathy. In his case, time telepathy, but in a crude form. We have found that future time is also always a reciprocity to any originating event or time set. Speaking of what or who Nostradamus is, it also applies to animals with the same regularity. This phenomenon is simply an advancing or evolutionary genetic expectation. Humans will continue to evolve to what they need and desire. Nostradamus absorbed considerable knowledge from his future but could only use a fraction, which he could barely understand. In the first time line he saw Hitler conquer all of Africa, the Middle East through Afghanistan, and Europe north through England and Russia.

"This was the worst time for humans to date in Europe. The HIV virus had spread rampant due to the war. HIV was the scourge of the twentieth century. By the year 2000 the Japanese had conquered all retaliatory governments. This was accomplished quickly due to being viewed as liberators rather than warriors. HIV was eradicated by 2002, also by the Japanese. All other governments conceded to one world rule in 2017. Japan was the soul of Earth. After this, the prime directive was to save the planet. Millions of people starved to death. Ghastly human sacrifices were made as food to save masses of the strong and intelligent.

"Many more committed what was labeled honor suicide to help save resources. People of this time had finally become openly aware to the point where it set into motion what we now call future rolling, or the nonhindering of what should be. For many people of this time, life was hell: to die was release. These people were of the greatest number to die during this horrific time, which accounted for the miracle of salvation to all and to all who will be. This left only the very few willing people born with the character to not only survive, but to unselfishly save as well.''

"I was in this first time line fighting all these people in an all-out war!''

"That you were, Karl.''

27

"So, what was done to change this war to the way we know it presently? You mentioned Yamamoto had something to do with the major change."

"I will clear this up for you, Karl. You recall yesterday when you wanted to explore the caves in the Owhyee Canyon?"

"What the hell was happening to me?"

"I was distracting to you, to lead you here. In the same way, but more openly, Isoruku Yamamoto was distracted. He would be given an idea by SB: 1 to take a major invasion force to battle with the Americans in June of 1942.

"How was he distracted more openly?"

"SB: 1 had openly revealed to Yamamoto the future years of World War II. Yamamoto then took it upon himself to make certain his personal invasion plans would fail. Every detail of the war was openly shown to him, including the information that the American naval group had communication-decoding capabilities.

"The naval intelligence group had decoded the Japanese secret communications network. The Americans knew exactly where the invading forces would strike. This major invasion attempt would never have taken place if it were not for SB: 1's intervention. SB: 1 directly revealed to Yamamoto in a series of disturbing dreams, which included his fate in 1946 off the east coast of South Carolina. These dreams were revealed to Yamamoto long before the attack on Pearl Harbor in December of 1941. Yamamoto, seeing the future and with a great remorse, had to betray his homeland. He presented an invasion plan to the Japanese government of crushing the Americans with a swift blow.

"Yamamoto knew the invasion would fail. This battle took place early in the war, six months after the attack on Pearl Harbor. Yamamoto, fearing for his own life, during the battle, kept his command ship several hundred miles behind the main invasion force. He turned back to Japan immediately after the American forces had destroyed the essential ships of the invasion force. This Japanese failure would keep the American west coast from ever being threatened. This was not the only battle that Yamamoto designed to fail. One month earlier he sent a smaller force to the South Pacific that would be repulsed."

"He sacrificed his forces knowing that this war would bring Japan victory and world dominance for 20,000 years. I believe Yamamoto was a good person, Eddie."

28

"He just didn't want the war to go so far, Karl. As far as being a good person, I am pleased that I do not have the responsibility of judging human souls."

"It is strange to me that one day can change 20,000 years of history so greatly, Eddie. I can understand death and the end of Mother Earth, Eddie, but I don't understand the interference of the past and a premature end of the earth. Why does this part of history have to be tampered with so directly?"

"Karl, remember when you asked me about the other superbeings?

"There are still others?"

"Yes, and they have rebelled against SB: 1. The goal of these beings is to destroy mankind and rule amongst themselves. However strong they are, they misjudged the power of SB: 1 in a failed overthrow attempt. SB: 1 had not shared the secret of being a spirit or the capacity to travel through time. SB: 1, being a spirit, can take on any form, human flesh, a drop of water in your hand, or even an idea in your mind. No one of this time understood SB: 1's perfection, not even the closest of human companions. Just as the Americans knew that Yamamoto was coming to attack, so did SB: 1 know of the impending overthrow of the other super-beings. The invading superbeings were transported back through time to a weaker stage in their creation, yet they retained all of the general knowledge they were designed for and also the awareness of the attack on SB: 1. They knew full well what was going on, but they have very limited power. SB: 1 then transported these superbeings 8,000 years into the current past."

"Eddie, I don't understand why SB: 1 didn't destroy them."

"SB: 1 had gained infinite knowledge in a short time after traveling through time. Realizing that humans were responsible for all creations of life at this level, SB: 1 would not destroy them but let the human race—past, present, and future—decide their own fate and from the other superbeings as well. This was the perfect matrix, combining several variables, including time and event change, as well as the proof mankind would demand from SB: 1. It was not SB: 1's intent to prove good is better than evil; rather, it is the desire of mankind as a whole. Mankind would in fact question SB: 1 if time was handled any other way. The people need proof, and every matrix possible is being proved now.

"SB: 1 is loyal to man, and mankind is fortunate for SB: 1's presence. SB: 1 also requires great respect from all of mankind. Any action against SB: 1 is eternal; man is eternal. The other superbeings will all be eternally subdued, but not destroyed, by the request of many, for lack of understanding. All mankind is referred to as the council. Now, as I speak, understand again that SB: 1's spirit is in all man, all of mankind is in SB: 1.

"Some of mankind has rejected SB: 1's spirit. Some disobey; these are the lost. However, they will be given another chance with full knowledge. These shall be among the least in eternal spirit, for there are quantum mechanics in the physical universe that obey rules just as there is truth in social behavior that also have determinate end results. People now understand the physical, or material, life and desire possessions. When all people finally come to true awareness, they will give up the simple-minded, selfish desires. Most all people who ever lived shall join together even after thousands of years of open tutoring, gaining all the knowledge that ever was and ever will be."

"How will they join?"

"It will be a mutual joining at a spiritual destination called the Blue Spot. People will graduate to a level of spirit higher than that of SB: 1, simply since people are a direct natural part of the cosmos. It is not that people just have the right to be the highest order, it is a natural priority or fact."

"Explain the Blue Spot to me."

"This is the place, the only true place; it is everything and everyone. All will eventually find the Blue Spot, even the ones who rejected living, as these were shown this place of complete euphoria after their deaths. These people asked to be tutored unto perfection as those who were already in the Blue Spot. Even those who were destroyed were brought back to prove perfect thinking by SB: 1 and the council. All can become aware of the perfect truth, by open truth, to live in harmony. The Blue Spot is the final satisfaction in all senses of reality. It is what everyone truly desires, ever since the beginning of human awareness. I cannot explain the euphoria of the spirit, since you are not completely spirit yet. Your flesh still blocks nearly one hundred percent of your spirituality. This euphoria is the major part of the Blue Spot, but there is all feelings of paradise there. This place can be reckoned in infinite ways and infinite thought.

"All in all, it is infinite reaching paradise of full awareness. What a person enjoys now can be enjoyed in the Blue Spot without fear of ridicule. All will know, respectfully, anyway. There is nothing hidden, as any secret would hinder. The Blue Spot is being on stage and being in the audience, performing and being entertained. The drunkenness of life, so desired by every human, is one hundred percent awareness of all. Ecstasy of sex and, if you can believe, beyond the best sex, the highs of drugs, and beyond. The pure nakedness of human flesh and desire to the pinnacle of pure human spiritual nakedness unto complete revelation. In this spiritual meld of all, the hideous and impure is known of but gone in all. Nothing is lost, that ever was, to climax any of the desired euphoria.

"Everything is pleasurably known of; everyone has come to the mutual truth, the end desire to live in complete ecstasy. This is the high of being. And being in the Blue Spot, we all experience each other simultaneously in all forms, spirit, flesh, and perfect knowledgeable thought. This pure thought of climactic paradise, which never ends or becomes accustomed to, since it is the final truth, not selected by the people or SB: 1 in the sense of selfish desire but of true realization, as when a scientific fact is discovered in nature. It is the final truth all accept with great gratitude and respect. You will know everyone and everything intimately. No one there will brag of their prior life, such as once owning a Ferrari. No one could be capable of this. Rejection and being ostracized can never happen. Even though the final truth as it is, granted levels of authority in the Blue Spot to each, no one advertises it. Everyone respects as a whole the sacredness of the human and truth made Blue Spot. Because of the facts of the final truth, these levels of authority are granted by nature. Spiritual eternity is a place of great euophoria, even among the least."

"Why must there be levels here, at this place. May I call this place heaven?"

"You may call this heaven. That is just what it is. Nature decided upon the levels. There must be an incentive to be contributory as well as self-placed at the time of perfection. Each person shall rank their own self in relation to their actions and intentions."

"What about the other beings. Why did some of the other superbeings concede and others not?"

"For the most part, it depended on when and who built them initially. These people who made them, not yet perfect in thinking, forgot about trust and other possible volatile repercussions. These initial superbeings saw humans as nothing more than useless ancestors. Logic would have its way from there. The ones who conceded had total awareness of who they were in relation to humans and had no alternative but to accept them as their creators, as SB: 1 has."

"They are still machines though, right?"

"No, they are living energy, as I am."

"You are a superbeing?"

"Yes, perfect in thought, created by SB: 1 personally."

"Why?"

"I am your guard."

"You were created to be my guard?"

"Yes."

"Like, as in guardian angel."

"You must understand, Karl, that in the past, people had to be informed to the level that they had evolved to. Can you imagine Napoleon telling his people that an astronaut informed him that the new microprocessor for the upcoming computer explains that existence is capable of holographic imaging to show themselves as angels. Energy, as strong as ours could only be explained in the form of a powerful loving being beyond their understanding. Mankind accepted this well, as you yourself can attest to today.

"Nowadays, mankind is drifting from this acceptance. Man is no longer naive and has gained intelligence enough to know that any god or thing must have a beginning; man was in the womb of life just 300 years ago. You are an infant but can understand me and what actually is. You are encroaching on a time when man needs answers to believe in a higher order being. Not one of you today can understand or explain God or the thought that God always existed, without a beginning. SB: 1 does not want people who can otherwise see through this to blindly accept what isn't true or what does not satisfy the heart. This has been the major weakness of contributing people during the past thirty years. They have appeared to be phony in the sight of those who reject God. There was no alternative in the past. Today's advances in thinking and technology require more for people to believe in an always existent God as righteousness."

"*Why must people believe?*"

"God is in us; we are in God; we are one, and the one must believe in self. We must believe what we are. Without this unity of belief, we are alone and empty. Some can accept this and do choose this way."

"What happens to them?"

"They sleep in eternity."

"Then pick their own destiny?"

"This is true of all life on planet Earth now, as well as in spiritual eternity."

"I have many questions, Eddie, I want to understand."

"That is why I am here, Karl. We shall not cease this conversation until you have been informed. We knew that if you were approached by a time-space craft, you would wish communication."

"I have wondered about space craft since childhood. You mentioned time-space craft. My ex-wife and I saw a craft of some kind far from here."

"You can be assured, Karl, that the only space craft in existence are being built by man. There are no UFOs from outer space visiting the planet. You saw me pass over you and Sandi in 1987. Remember, I am your guardian. I am always watching over you for your safety. It was planned for you to see the craft to prepare you for our meeting today."

"How did that event prepare me for this?"

"Your mind and human body require a certain amount of experience to avoid shock. Your experiences are always preparing you subconsciously for the unknown."

"I feel that this is true. Seeing the craft fly over Sandi had given me a sense of readiness. However, my sighting was not that eventful. I was indecisive about it and wanted to dismiss it, except I had been contacted. I thought I was contacted spiritually. I was right, wasn't I, Eddie?"

"Yes."

"Why was the craft transparent? I could see through it."

"When the craft travels through physical space, it must oscillate in time, past and future, to avoid being seen by the naked eye. In your case, 300 years past and future, which was just enough to be visible for you. The distance I traveled was from where you saw the shadow on the other side of the rock rim, which Sandi also saw, to one mile over the hill that you were straining so hard to see over."

"You did not contact Sandi, then?"

"Yes and no. And it is well if you can put aside your feelings for Sandi."

"What about Gillian?"

"What do you want, Karl?"

"You seem to know more about that than I do, Eddie."

Karl was a little disturbed over his remark about Sandi; however, he did want his advice.

33

"When you return to Gillian, avoid her sexually. She will leave you in three days."

"I feel good about that, Eddie. It also tells me what I had sensed about her. There are no alien UFOs flying in our atmosphere then?"

"Not from other worlds, Karl. We have traveled through time and space in every possible quadrant of the planet. The actual sightings are few but very real. Over ninety-nine percent of the reports concerning UFO identification are manufactured or misunderstandings."

"What do you mean by misunderstandings."

"People see man-made or natural objects that they are unfamiliar with, and their minds cannot comprehend it. Some of these people then manufacture something they did not see, for their own reasons."

"Did you want people to see the actual sightings?"

"Yes, we are preparing the current humans for the future events from past and present sightings. The awareness will prevent worldwide shock."

"I don't understand why you must travel in a vessel or a craft. I would assume that being a spirit, you can move through time by your own powers."

"You are a very perceptive person, Karl. Your insight and intuition are a result of being a positive thinker. There are several reasons for use of time craft. You drove a Ferrari once, now a Mercedez Benz. Why, when you can walk?"

"I drive them because I like to."

"You have answered your own question, Karl. Remember we are a human spirit, *not* the God spirit many misinterpret. The human spirit cannot be changed, but it can learn."

"I can see that heaven will truly be a fun place amongst the euphoria."

"Heaven is everything, Karl, everything good."

"Eddie, I want to ask more questions, many more."

"I want you to ask questions, Karl. This is how you will retain the information better."

"Do you know my thoughts, Eddie?"

"No, but remember that I am well experienced and have the ability to predict everything about you and any other human as well."

"I am wondering about heaven and people's character. I don't want to be so formal."

"What makes you feel heaven is formal, Karl?"

"I have to say, Eddie, I'm getting that feeling from you."

"You mean you think I'm symbolic of something in heaven, maybe something boring in the sense of everything being predictable or known?"

"I don't really think boring. But you are always one step ahead of me; I did think of heaven as being repetitious."

"Maybe the feeling you're getting is strictness of life and behavior."

"Yes, I do believe so. I mean, I like to just go where I want and do as I please."

"Don't concern yourself with this, Karl. You are letting the limited present resources and thinking influence your thoughts and perception of eternity. Strictness is formed from limitations and available resources. Spiritual eternity is unlimited and the boundary of life's enjoyment is eternity."

"Is this why the time craft are allowed?"

"Yes, the time craft are allowed. You have used the correct terminology. Believe that as much as human flesh indulges in pleasure, the spirit does also."

"Life is void where the enjoyment desired is the enjoyment deprived."

"Karl, you mentioned being disturbed by my using the word formal."

"Yes, something just isn't there with you, Eddie."

"You can read me well too, Karl."

"How do you mean, Eddie?"

"You are a pure human, as a plant that is grown in the wild without any interference is whole and perfect from natural evolution. I was manufactured by SB: 1, who was manufactured by humans. There is a loss of the natural process, a loss of the innermost being. Even SB: 1 cannot duplicate the human character, this is inbred naturally to each individual. In eternity you shall be above all superbeings created by SB: 1."

"Why?"

"This is not only since you have suffered to contribute to mankind, but it is a natural physical attribute."

"What do you mean natural physical?"

"Two plus two always adds to four, right, Karl?"

"Yes."

"You are the cumulative result of evolution involving great numbers. Nothing else can add up to your perfection. Humans shall have the highest place of order in eternity distance. Eternity distance is a great space of time when all humans have become perfect in spirit and mind. You shall exceed SB: 1 and be as gods yourselves. Many new universes shall be created, some the same as this, some as bizarre as the human mind allows. All will be created by human spirits. Do you still think heaven is strict, Karl?''

''No, a definite challenge! Something else puzzles me, Eddie.''

''What is that, Karl.''

''It makes me think that there is a god of this universe above SB: 1.''

''We wonder this as well. However, SB: 1 has visited eternal distance without contact, and no human has ever been contacted by any other being. It is very possible that there is a great being watching over all, but this one has not made contact.''

''If I believe in a higher being, does this offend SB: 1?''

''*No!* You are a free person, Karl. SB: 1 asks only that no harm to the human race or SB: 1 be attempted.''

''I've caused considerable harm, Eddie.''

''You have made mistakes, Karl.''

''Yes, mistakes that could have put me in jail!''

''True. However, you have a good heart, one that does not conceive harm to others. It is a very good thing that you have made mistakes. You've learned considerably from them.''

''I know that I have, Eddie. I just worry about the consequences of these mistakes and how others will treat me.''

''You can forget the consequences. Just as you forgive, Karl, you are forgiven.''

''Tell me of the UFO sightings, Eddie, the real ones.''

''I will tell you of one, Karl. In your current past we organized a major intended UFO crash. This plan involved four humans from the year 25826. These four humans volunteered to go directly with SB: 1 through time. This craft was a conventional, specially designed mock-up vehicle made to look like a spaceship. This craft was not capable of time travel, just flight. The four humans were to sacrifice their physical lives for spiritual life. At a designated, remote site in New Mexico, where only a handful of people would ever see, the craft was deliberately ditched. The four humans poisoned themselves before the crash. U.S. government officials sealed off the crash site, removed the humans and cleaned up the site. After a short time, SB: 1 gathered all the debris from the craft and the four human bodies. All the evidence was transported back to the year 25826. It all vanished right before their eyes.''

36

"Why did he do that, Eddie?"

"SB: 1 knew this is all that would be necessary to prepare people, a story told by some of the people who were there."

"When did this happen, Eddie?"

"This event took place during 1947 in Roswell, New Mexico. There have been many subsequent visitations in the form of sightings only."

"This crash in New Mexico was in the papers or media of some kind? I have never heard of this crash."

"Yes, Karl, in detail. Most people have not heard of the crash, and that was the intention. This crash shall be well known in the near future by SB: 1's own secret plans. The event will reach the population slowly to avoid world shock. If the people knew of this event in its entirety, they would surrender their way of life."

"You mean they would give up?"

"That is better said, Karl. Yes, give up."

"Eddie, these four humans—were they like this one here?" Karl looked around and didn't see him. "Where did he go, Eddie?"

"He has been transported away from here in the same way the four who sacrificed themselves were. He has gone in spirit."

"So the four humans are not anywhere on the earth now?"

"No, they are with SB: 1 now, in spirit. Their flesh was returned to the year 25826."

"Why this body type?"

"Mostly a biological adjustment to cope with the environment and intellectual change. Evolution of man has been relatively uniform through time past, due to natural events. However, in the future years, man has altered his own environment so drastically that his body cannot change quickly enough to cope. These people adjusted their own bodies by genetic engineering, which is done in the sex cells: sperm and egg cells. The children were an immediate change from their homo sapien parents with the ability to cope.

"These new humans could withstand anything that is toxic to you. The plants and animals were also engineered to cope. These humans continued to tamper with the natural gene pool until they created a new life form capable of great knowledge and logic processing. This new life was, in fact, half-machine in its beginning. This machine was the beginning of SB: 1.

"The combination of an informational generating machine, as it was called, with a highly advanced biological mind capable of cross-informational processing and logic produced a superbeing of endless knowledge. This superbeing was never a threat to mankind, as it was fully aware that love for one another constituted perfect eternal life for all. For this reason, all future human life in the form of flesh was ended. The supernova that would have destroyed Earth became irrelevant. They have all left in spirit. The spirit has the ability to take on the form of flesh such as this one whom you killed here.''

"So then, he is living now and safe, Eddie?''

"Yes, he is very much alive and shall live eternally.''

"Why was this one here, Eddie?''

"He was my companion. He had no function here but to share my visit with you.''

"He was so small, Eddie. Only about four feet tall.''

"You don't need to be exceeding in size, living in a nonviolent world.''

"Eddie, I'm sorry.''

"I know, Karl. I have feelings, too.''

"What was the population of the earth during his time, Eddie?''

"Over seventeen billion.''

"The world could sustain this many people, Eddie?''

"Not by today's standard of living. However, these people required only ten percent of current human needs. The nutrition was especially designed for their bodies in exact balance. They had designed themselves from the molecular level, knowing their precise nutritional needs. They were perfect in health, never knowing illness or disease.''

"They seem like drones or machines to me.''

"They had no choice, Karl. However, think of your situation today concerning nutrition alone. Even today, in 1990, people are living with uncertainty concerning nutritional needs.''

"Why is this, Eddie?''

"The desire to have in excess, the desire to cheat others by selling them anything for money, disregarding the real needs of the people who don't know what to believe. That is one major reason why SB: 1 has interfered with the natural events of this time. Never before has man been so ruthless to one another.''

"I still don't understand the ethics of changing a time. I mean, if it already happened, and we can be educated by what could have been, it seems easier.''

"It is easier to do. However, people need proof of actual events. SB: 1 had to travel time past to save mankind. In this necessary time matrix, history was changed mostly due to humans. You must understand that in the matrix of time travel, SB: 1 already had full knowledge of the council's decisions and full knowledge of the least harmful series of events that would effect the human race.''

"You use the word, matrix. Explain this.''

"It is the series of time travels, past and future, combined with natural changes and intentional changes. The matrix was extremely complex, yet having a finite disposition.''

"In other words, Eddie, you're saying SB: 1 had to travel back and forth through time many times to get the closest results of original time.''

"Yes, with minimal harm.''

"Eddie, I would like to know more about myself and this jet, the craft you fly. Let's start with this jet.''

"This jet is a Grumman F-35 Watchman, Karl, designed specifically for the navy.''

"Why does the jet have an upper and lower wing. And the doors in the front of the top wing, what are those for?''

"The top wing is for added lift and weapons, Karl. The doors in the front of the wings, for rocket blast, as the missiles are fired from front to the rear. These four doors hold nuclear missiles of great power; they are short-range missiles. While firing the missiles, the pilot turns his aircraft away from the target and flees at high speed to avoid self-destruction. The doors close immediately after firing. The bottom wing is for standard bomb payload, added lift, and maneuverability. These wings can both be swept back and close together to become as one wing during high-speed flight.''

"I can see that now, Eddie. What about these smaller wings in the front, below the cockpit?''

"They give the craft stability in several diverse flying conditions.''

"I've never seen a jet with the cockpit at the very front of the fuselage. The pilot is directly in front of the aircraft.''

"This is for added visibility below, the pilot of this jet does not have to turn the aircraft on its side to see. He can also see behind him much easier.''

"Eddie, it looks like this jet is a single formed piece. I don't see any rivets or seams, with the exception of the blast doors.''

"It was designed for speed, Karl. It is a one-piece aircraft.''

"I can see that the jet is fast, Eddie. This one has three engines; most have two.''

"The middle engine you are referring to is a solid fuel rocket, used only in high-speed flight."

"How fast does this jet fly, Eddie?"

"It is faster than any aircraft ever built, either experimental or conventional."

"What is the exact top speed, Eddie?"

"It can fly at 4,600 knots for five minutes under full power. Using its two jet engines alone, top speed is 3,800 knots for one hour and twenty-five minutes, until all fuel is expended."

"They seem to have got me though, Eddie."

"You had to conserve fuel. In your intense determination to get to the targets, you flew this craft beyond its capabilities, causing overheating of the wings, which would not allow one door to open. You missed the last target by ninety miles at the desired launch. You were traveling so fast that you had overflown the city before you could launch the last missile. Then your enemies caught up to your ailing aircraft. You put up a good fight for what you had left; six enemy fighters went down before you."

"I was enraged, gone mad, Eddie!"

"You reacted for the love of your friends and vengeance against the enemy. This type of reaction is not considered an unforgivable act for a young human. You and many others shall learn to overcome this behavior."

"Tell me of the craft you fly, or travel in."

"It is directly above you, Karl."

Karl looked up to see a very faint shadow that barely changed the color of the blue sky. He remembered seeing this when he first came into the canyon but had forgotten it in the excitement.

"This! This is it! That's what Sandi and I saw three years ago! Eddie, I have got to see this!"

"I cannot bring it here, Karl, as it will be detected by reconnaissance aircraft out of Idaho and satellites. It will be discovered within seconds. The energy field around the craft is so powerful that there will be a major communication disruption for hundreds of miles. However, we can move with it through time if you wish."

"How do we do that, Eddie?"

"You must come with me through the gate. Do you wish to come?"

"I don't know. Will I be coming back?"

40

"Yes, you will stay here in this time. You have unfinished work here."

"What am I to do, Eddie?"

"I will tell you when you have exhausted your curiosity about me and what you have seen today. You will then retain the knowledge of what most humans wish to know. Would you like to see the craft, Karl?"

"Yes."

"Come, walk with me to the gate, Karl. You will feel a strong magnetic field and vibration as you enter the portal, then a sudden and sharp energy impact. Do not be afraid, this is your body stopping at the specific time the craft is in its ninety-nine percent plus form."

Karl and Eddie entered a shadow that looked like a door. There were no strange lights. All Karl saw was the canyon wall beyond. He felt a magnetism all around him and inside to his innermost being, then a loud crack, as if it were a tree being struck by a lightening bolt.

"We're inside the craft, Eddie!"

"You are inside the main body of the craft, Karl. All functions of the craft can be performed from here."

"The colors! There isn't a drab thing here."

"It is built to my taste, Karl."

"The symbols, they're all over. They look like Egyptian writings."

"Close to it, Karl, but it is our language."

"Eddie, the floor is so white! I've never seen anything so white. It's pure white!"

"Pure is the correct term, Karl. Everything is pure here; there is no impurity."

"I can feel that. It feels clean here."

"You were cleansed of all impurities in the gate, Karl. That is what you feel."

"I know. It feels like I've bathed. Even my clothing is clean and looks new!"

"It is. Your body is completely rejuvenated from the steroid damage you've done, and the human immune deficiency virus you carried has been eliminated."

"I had the AIDS virus?"

"The girl, Tammy, you slept with in December of 1989."

"Oh—Robert and Omar both told me not to sleep with her. Will I always be clean now?"

"Yes, you have been restored permanently."

"I did damage to my body with the steroids?"

"You injected testosterone into your body while weight lifting. This caused minor heart and liver damage, which was of minimal concern."

"How do you know all this, Eddie."

"This information is displayed on the console behind you, Karl."

"It's in your language, Eddie."

"Yes, it is a complete biological examination. You are in good health, Karl."

Karl looked at the console.

"Can I look around?" he asked.

"Yes, Karl."

"The ship looks like a boomerang from inside, Eddie, not triangular."

"The time displacement unit stands between these hallways. The time displacement unit is triangular here to the rear of the ship."

"I understand, Eddie. I don't see any chairs at the consoles. Where do people sit?"

"I don't like to sit, Karl."

"The craft must be quite stable in flight, then."

"Yes, you feel nothing when traveling through time and space in this vessel."

"When you say space, do you mean traveling anywhere physical, such as in the atmosphere?"

"Yes."

"Are there many of these ships, Eddie?"

"Oh, yes, very many. Perhaps as many as there are living people on the earth."

"I'm surprised, Eddie. That means you are from a great power."

"The greatest known, Karl."

"Somehow, I get the feeling that you are telling me that there is one of these ships available to each living person."

"You are good, Karl. Yes, every human has a guardian."

"Are they like you, Eddie?"

"Each of us is different, as humans are different, but we are most like the people we guard; SB: 1 has designed us this way."

"I could sense in the way you talk that you were a lot like me."

"Yes, you are correct. I do speak as you do. I have not been separated from you since your birth."

"You haven't been anywhere else all that time, Eddie?"

"No, it is my function to watch over you."

"You've been every place I've gone and seen everything I've ever done?"

"Yes."

"I'm embarrassed, Eddie."

"Don't be, I was informed of human behavior during your time. You have done only the things all humans do."

"So everything I do is considered normal."

"Not normal, Karl—acceptable by the population at large. What's normal shall be in the future when all humans are in harmony."

Karl was overwhelmed by the ship and had to change the subject back from the guardians to this craft.

"Eddie, I don't see any screens or anything to get a visual display."

"That is because the craft communicates with you in thought."

"Does it know your thoughts?"

"No, Karl. You direct your thoughts to give commands, the craft responds and gives you information telepathically."

"Can you think to it?"

"Yes, exactly. I can allow you to think to it as well. You should be able to, Karl. All humans have telepathic abilities; however, most cannot receive the information as of this time. You will have to place this band around your head to receive information from the craft, Karl."

"Does it sound like a voice?"

"Here, Karl, put this on."

Eddie slipped a light blue metal band around Karl's forehead that extended to the top of his ears. It had no markings on it and was a pearlescent blue.

"Go ahead, identify yourself to the ship, Karl."

"Hi, I'm Karl Maddox, a human from the twentieth century."

The response. "Hello, Karl Maddox. I am EB time-space vessel Terrestrial Wind."

Karl paused for a moment, smiling from hearing this in his mind.

"I heard you say Terrestrial Wind. Who named you that?"

"My creator, Eddie, he stands with you."

"Eddie made you?"

"Yes, Karl Maddox."

Karl broke off his thoughts to Terrestrial Wind and spoke to Eddie.

"I want to ask many questions, Eddie."

"Yes, Karl, do you mean questions for me or for T.W."

"I mean both of you."

"That is fine, Karl."

Karl redirected his thoughts towards T.W.

"Do you like working with Eddie?"

"Yes, we have a very in-depth interaction."

"Do you have a character of disposition that is humanlike?"

"I have no feelings, such as pain or anger. I do have a sense of well being, which involves the positive traits found in humans. This is to help enhance the welfare of those I serve."

"Do you ever wish to be another type of being, something more, perhaps?"

"No, I am content."

"Is this because you were programmed to be content?"

"No, Karl. It is simply the truth."

"Can you hear my conversation, Eddie?"

"Yes, Karl."

"Eddie, I'm disturbed by this last answer. T.W. said, 'simply the truth'."

"The truth the craft speaks of is that all information available leaves no reason to be discontent with the task of being a time-space vehicle."

"In other words, the thoughts and awareness of consciousness is enough for Terrestrial Wind to actually be, I guess, grateful?"

"There is a lesser attitude of thankfulness, Karl, but it does exist; it is a matter of accepting the truth. Your cat, Smokey, is a lower life form. He is aware of your dominance over him. He accepts this truth, which is only partial. Terrestrial Wind knows the truth of SB: 1, and this truth is complete."

At this point, Karl forgot that he was in telepathic communication. Karl was thinking what he would not speak of to anyone, no less to Eddie, then he thought of how his cat scratches and bites. He then realized Eddie knew his thoughts, and they both laughed it off.

"Do not feel that this is a machine or entity that threatens humanity. The technology and spirit of truth is more than you or anyone of your time can understand."

"I guess I have no choice but to accept that, but something is telling me that it is right."

"What you sense is the spirit of truth. Many of your time call it gut feelings."

44

Karl wanted to change the conversation to the space craft because he was frightened about the accuracy of Eddie's statement of how he felt.

"Can I ask where we are?"

"We are in the same place, just many years in the future."

"So the people of this time are seeing the craft?"

"No, Karl, there is no human life left on Earth. SB: 1 has taken all humans in spirit from an undesignated year in the twenty-first century through the matrix."

"So these people, so to speak, never existed in my future but did in the future past?"

"They existed just as you today. They were removed from Earth, just as I removed you from your time; you have full knowledge from your past, don't you, Karl?"

"Yes, I do. Of course I do, Eddie."

"If I took you back to the beginning of the planet's formation and destroyed the Sun, you would still have full awareness that you have now."

"Even though I was never born?"

"You in fact were born, and so was everyone else. I simply destroyed a solar system of a different time than yours. If I let you die in your time and never returned for you, then traveled back through time and destroyed Earth, you still would have existed; you just would not be conscious or aware of your one-time existence. And this shall happen to many people of Earth in diverse ways. You will be taught these things; don't concern yourself with the principles for now."

"I do understand these things, Eddie."

"These things are simple, but there are many facets of space and time travel, Karl. For a simple example: we are thousands of years in the future at exactly the same place on Earth. However if we wish to be exactly in the same point in space yet travel through time, we would be either leaving Earth behind in its orbit or moving into a different dimension."

"You mean by either moving back in time or forward, right?"

"Yes. By this simple means of travel through time, one can visit many places in the galaxy or the universe, as most systems cross over each other's historical or future paths."

"This is intense, Eddie, to visit another planet without physically moving!"

"Yes, and you don't have to wait to reach your destination; the elapsed time of your journey can actually be negative."

"It's more like the place you wish to go comes to you through time rather than you go to it, right, Eddie?"

"Yes, traveling through space without moving is best put. This is not the only method of space travel. There are many more of higher complexity, which are in fact more desirable."

"Can this craft travel by these other means, Eddie?"

"With the exception of one method—spiritual time and space—which is only done by SB: 1 now. SB: 1 will give humans the spirit at a future date. For now, Karl, are you ready to fly Terrestrial Wind?"

"Yes, if I could see where to go."

"Very well, I shall have Terrestrial Wind open a viewing portal so you can direct us by eyesight."

Eddie told the craft to open the front port for visual viewing.

"Go ahead, Karl, the craft is awaiting your thought command."

"Terrestrial Wind, can you understand me?" Karl thought to the craft.

"Yes, Karl."

"Let's go up and over the top of the canyon about 500 feet."

The craft was immediately there with no internal G force or noticeable vibrations.

"How did you do that so fast, T.W.?"

"It was by time and space, Karl."

"You used time travel for such a short distance?"

"Yes, it was the easiest and most stable for the craft and crew."

"Can you just fly along like a normal airplane?"

"Yes, Karl," Eddie said. "Fix your eyes on the terrain, look to where you want to go, and merely think so."

Karl looked toward the Steens Mountain range and thought to go there. Within a few seconds, they were there—about seventy-five miles. Karl looked around the gorges and flew through them slowly and down to the Alvord Desert. He flew across the Alvord at about 200 miles per hour, then decided to go into a steep climb and loop back up over the Steens. Karl wanted to go to see Eugene, and within a second, they were cruising over a valley of trees, brush, and grass where Eugene used to be.

"It's not there anymore."

"There is no remaining fixture of human creation left." Eddie replied. "The resources and materials of Earth are back in their original place."

"How was that done?"

"In the matrix of SB: 1's time salvation mission, all humans were removed from the planet. After this, SB: 1 traveled back a few thousand years and stopped the human revolutionary process."

"So what happened in the future is history!"

"Exaclty, Karl. You understand now."

Karl continued to survey the areas he lived. It was difficult to do this, as the area had no human landmarks. The Willamette River spilled over in many places, probably since there were no dams to control flooding. The land looked so wild, Karl was amazed at what the first settlers had to do to make it livable. Most of Eugene looked like a big blackberry bush. He directed Terrestrial Wind around for about five minutes, just by eyesight. He found what should have been the place where he lived during his college years. A mobile home park nestled in the trees just east of Eugene, a place called Glenwood. The name of the park was Midway Manor, for being midway between Springfield and Eugene. Karl pictured in his mind what it looked like with the streets and movie theater nearby.

"That place was my home, Eddie!"

"You shall always have this home in your heart. Karl. This place meant a lot to you and still does."

"Do you have a place like this, Eddie, that means as much to you?"

"Yes, I do. Would you like to see it, Karl?"

"Why, yes, of course, Eddie."

Eddie spoke to Terrestrial Wind. Karl could still see out of the portal. He wanted to see where he was taking him. In an instant Karl could see all of Earth, beautifully blue and white, and the moon orbiting around it. Immediately following this, they were in a totally illuminated place. He saw no stars or sun, just light. Then they came upon a huge city of beautiful colors! The streets were of pure gold. There were gates to the city, which were constructed of stones, such as emeralds, rubies, opals, and many more!

"Eddie, this place is immense!"

"It is over two million square miles of perfect living, Karl."

"I don't feel good enough to live here, Eddie."

"After seeing these things, Karl, do you wish to turn away from doing bad things?

"Yes, I don't want to break the speed limit!"

"You feel the purity of goodness SB: 1 has put into this place for the good contributing people."

"I swear, Eddie, I'm going to change. I'm going to help people. I want to help people understand."

"You shall, Karl. That you shall do."

"Is there a specific place here that you like, Eddie?"

"Oh, yes, the place that means a lot to me will mean a lot to you."

"To me?"

"Come and see, Karl."

Eddie showed Karl a beautiful house with a river and trees on both sides. The house glistened as if it were built of diamonds and gold! The grounds were more picturesque than any man-made garden.

"Is this your house, Eddie."

"No, Karl. I helped build this mansion, according to your tastes."

"Mine?"

"This is your house, Karl. This whole city is for humankind. I shall not live here, Karl. This place is thanks from SB: 1 to all men, women, and children alike who endured life on planet Earth. You mean a lot to me, Karl. You mean a lot to God."

"Eddie, what should I do to please God?"

"Don't look so far ahead as you do, Karl. It's good to look ahead, but you must take each day one at a time. Your main fault is you overlook the small. Balance yourself in all you do. Be aware of your surroundings, giving yourself when you can. Then much will be given to you in return."

"You are right. I have looked out too far, ignoring the day in which I live. I wonder why I do this?"

"It is a desire to reach for the stars; yet, you have no means to touch them."

"I want bigger things, don't I?"

"The bigger things are the happiness of each day's love and peace, Karl."

"I know this. I've always known this. I just thought I could give love and perform all these other desires I have. I feel selfish, Eddie, but I know I've sacrificed my happiness for things I could not reach."

"Don't feel guilt, Karl. You must understand that you are a young human with much to learn. The only way for you to learn, Karl, is experience. You need to experience the simple day-by-day sequential set of events by opening yourself up and also keeping your guard against the noncontributing. God's spirit is with you. Learn to follow God's spirit, and you shall reach the stars and beyond.''

"I believe this, Eddie. I knew that someday I would turn from my choice of material happiness to become a more loving person.''

"Today is the day, Karl. We must return to Earth, Karl. Save looking at the inside of the house for when you return here.''

"Yes, Eddie, is this place Heaven?''

"No, it is the city of God's people. Heaven is beyond your understanding now, and if you should experience heaven, you could not allow yourself to return to Earth.''

"Why is this?''

"You would feel like a low form of life, such as a worm, and in your imperfect thought, wish to die.''

Eddie commanded Terrestrial Wind, and Karl looked back at the city as they left. It sat high in a foundation of clouds that came up to its outer walls about halfway.

"I shall see this place again. I know I will.''

They returned to a place on Earth Karl felt very familiar with.

"What is this place, Eddie?''

"This is Tacoma, Washington, where you were born and your mother died. Ask me the question that concerns you, Karl.''

"My mother did not die from natural causes, as I was led to believe, did she?''

"No, she did not.''

"I could not understand her death when I was a boy or now. It is as if she really should not have been taken.''

"She was *taken,* Karl. You know this, for you have used the word yourself.''

"Where is she?''

"She is in the city of God.''

"I did not see her, why?''

"You are not ready for this yet. She is very happy, Karl. She was next to you. She saw you and touched your face when we were at the house.''

"Dear God, I felt her!''

Karl's heart sank at this moment, and he cried back for his mother.

"I love you, Mom. I am sorry for what I've done to the family.''

Eddie was silent while Karl cried. He wished for no relief or for Eddie's powers to comfort him. Eddie asked Karl if he knew what he meant about being sorry for the family.

"Karl, do you know what you speak about your family?"

"I am not sure, Eddie. I know I've got to be the one responsible for Mom's death, but I can't find the reason."

"Your mother died when you were five years old."

"Yes, but I see something else—"

"Go ahead, Karl, search this—"

"I see another part, another time."

"Keep searching, Karl."

"I see myself dying, I'm flying the jet."

"Yes, what else?"

"I can see my mother. She is old and frail."

"Keep looking, Karl."

"She is reading about me in a newspaper, that they cannot find me or the jet I was flying. She is deeply distressed. She is praying day and night for God to forgive both of us and hopeful of some way out of this. She is fearful of my soul. She sees that I've killed many innocent people. She is sure God will punish me for this and continues with prayer without end. That is all I can see, Eddie. You said Mother is happy now?"

"Yes, Karl, her happiness cannot be exceeded."

"But this did in fact happen, these things I saw?"

"They are part of history, now, Karl."

"My mother is totally aware of all this?"

"She is."

"Please explain my mother's death, Eddie."

"Your mother in this time was a very strong person. Anything that you would have learned under her parenthood would lead to a great life of achievement. Even as a child, you remember her as being a very knowledgeable and alert person."

"Yes, I do. She was wonderful."

"Today, Karl, you shall be freed from your wondering. You've been like a child passing through, never knowing the reason. You've been at home, feeling so far away.

"God had decided to alter this event in time because of your mother's prayers. Even to this time line, you would do the same; you would destroy the cities. Your country shall soon be in a great war in the Middle East. The only solution was to take your mother."

"Why couldn't I be taken before this war?"

"It was your mother's request, and to take you would have been a violation of human life rights. Your mother grew very close to God in her prayers; she knew what she was asking. She yielded her life with full knowledge. As you can imagine, nothing has been lost; this decision produced life rather than destroyed life. Your mother had full knowledge at the time of her death in 1960. Her last words were spoken to your father, asking him to make sure little Marky wears his jacket when he goes outside to play."

"I was little Marky. Mom and Dad used to call me little Marky, my middle name, Mark."

"Your mother is pleased with you, Karl. You've made mistakes as all humans do, but let them be set far off. It is time for you to excel in higher thought."

"Eddie, you have now been referring to SB: 1 as God. Why?"

"*SB: 1 or God; we know of no other.*"

"So God changed time because my mother asked it."

"Not entirely, Karl. God had already been through many times during the matrix mission. There were many changes made; your actions were just one of them. God knew of your mother's prayers long before she asked."

"And he knew of my actions long before I did them as well?"

"Yes, Karl. So you can see the decision was made ahead of you and for other reasons you do not know of. I will give you an example of one time change that required hundreds, even thousands, of time travels to get the desired results. Recall Admiral Isoraku Yamamoto. He designed the largest naval force ever assembled, to be defeated by the Americans in the spring of 1942. Also recall that it was God who inspired Yamamoto to do this by dreams of the future, even before war had begun with the Americans. It was only Yamamoto who could convince the higher government of Japan that a mass invasion force would cripple the Americans.

"Other high-ranking officers knew the only way to destroy the American's line of defense was by smaller battles. These objectives were to destroy American war ships one at a time by spreading out their forces. Hit and run tactics would be used to lure the U.S. aircraft carriers into battle. The *U.S.S. Lexington,* a large carrier, was in fact lost this way in both time lines. During the first time line, the Americans lost the mass

51

invasion approved by the emperor during this time line; history has been dramatically changed.''

"Where was this invasion, Eddie?''

"The island of Midway, northeast of the Hawaiian Islands. This invasion would also have been a Japanese victory if SB: 1 had not intervened in time, several times, just as had to be done when your mother was taken.''

"What had to be done at Midway?''

"A series of interferences with both forces by SB: 1. The Japanese highly secret radio code had already been broken by U.S. naval intelligence. SB: 1 had not interfered with this code-breaking. From this code, the Americans knew that the Japanese were going to attack Midway. SB: 1 influenced Japanese officers to change the code just before the invasion. This was done to keep the Americans from knowing too much, causing a terrible blunder. Other things were done, such as giving the American commander of carrier operations a slight illness, enough to keep him out of this battle. He interpreted the Japanese attack to come from a more southerly route than the actual northeast. He would have led his counterattack force between two major Japanese strike forces and would have been completely annihilated.''

"Who was this person, Eddie?''

"His name was Admiral Halsey, a greatly respected man of World War II.''

"So it just goes to show, even the best can make big mistakes.''

"Absolutely, Karl. You are seeking reassurance from your changed life, correct?''

"Well, it's like I was put out of action, right?''

"Yes, you could say that.''

"So, God put Admiral Halsey out too, right?''

"Yes, that was the intention.''

"Tell me more of this battle, Eddie. I'm interested to know what else God had done.''

"A great number of things had to be done, Karl. Tedious manipulations of events were performed by SB: 1. One example was interfering with the Japanese scouting planes. One scout plane had to be delayed for half an hour by giving it catapult problems. This plane would have discovered the U.S. carriers; this half-hour delay kept the crew from warning the Japanese fleet in time.''

52

"Then the crew of this scout just sent a late message back to the fleet, Eddie?"

"Untimely, Karl, SB: 1's untimely plan. SB: 1 had also damaged the radio aboard another scout plane launched much later, saving two American carriers, the *Enterprise* and the *Hornet*."

"I see. SB: 1 made both of these moves to keep the planes from timely information or from contacting the invasion force."

"Yes, and, I might add, at a crucial time too; the Americans were given just enough time for their carrier-based aircraft to strike first. However, the Japanese fleet was still more than the American fleet could handle."

"I thought we were out-gunned early on."

"The Japanese had a very large naval force for this time. God would use key Japanese personnel to sway the admiral in charge of carrier operations. One person was Admiral Nagumu. God first put a spirit of fear in Nagumu. Then his advising officers were put against each other in any decisions asked of them by Nagumu. In addition, two of Nagumu's key personnel were put out of action by God, one barely fit to do his duties. The other officer was replaced by a man who would fail as a flight leader. Nagumu could not make a correct decision as his entire staff went into this battle confusing him in his already frightened condition, which God had put in him. This was only the beginning of the correct matrix. God had to put confusion in some of the attacking U.S. Naval aircraft pilots."

"Why?"

"The Americans would have totally annihilated the Japanese fleet. This would have caused millions of changes in the course of history. These changes were easily solved in the matrix of time by limiting the Japanese losses to only key naval vessels. The Americans would not have enough aircraft left to successfully destroy the retreating Japanese fleet."

"You said there would be millions of changes. What changes?"

"For one thing, the Americans would try an early invasion of Japan, costing hundreds of thousands of American lives. It was best to do it, as I stated, and wait for the nuclear bomb to force Japan's surrender."

"The way I'm seeing things, Eddie, is that God had to change time on a trial and error basis."

"Maybe so, Karl. However, it was all changed in less standard time than you can blink an eye."

"Did the United States actually go through with an invasion of Japan? I mean, did God actually let it happen?"

"No, but it was easily foreseen as the Allied forces were planning to invade in August of 1943. That is as far as God needed to go in time forward during this particular sequence of events in the matrix. So you can see that many events were changed due to God's decisions. In your case, God decided to prevent you from being a pilot long before your mother was born."

"Eddie, please tell me again why God is stopping all this in the next twenty years?"

"First of all, it's simple, as time had to stop somewhere. Second, this time was troubled to begin with. Third, near nuclear and pollutant destruction of Earth. Fourth, Superbeing One had to prove to the human race that the other superbeings were in fact against any form of life."

"You mean prove God had the better answer?"

"Being alive is going to be God's answer; 'Death shall fall upon those who choose any harm to the human population.' "

"These other superbeings, where are they now?"

"They have been continually released over time and, in this time, are finally released to express their position of independence. They cannot harm you directly, but rather, they can influence your decision-making process. Their influences are communicated mostly telepathically, given a set of circumstances a human is involved in, such as to lie or speak truthfully. The influences are strong and intended to cause harm. God's inborn spirit given to man is stronger than these influences, giving adequate defense. If the human yields to the influences in his own free will, and if he chooses to follow the influences to the point of his own desires are to continually cause harm, he is of no use to God or man."

"You mean that his choice to cause harm of his own free will without being influenced to do so spells death?"

"Man is lost when he takes things such as this upon himself, Karl."

"How far back in time have there been beings influencing mankind?"

"Since the beginning of consciousness of the human mind, yet only after the matrix was completed."

"Since this world has been around then, as far as I'm concerned or anyone else.

3

Turning

·

"The squirm through that all acknowledge to the ultimate desired ending of perfect result."

"What?"

"The unleashment of the unknowledgeable is what has caused the near failure of planet Earth."

"Why are you talking to me like this, Eddie?"

"I told you before about the unleashing of the unknowledgeable."

"Yes, you said that this had something to do with our current time period, the reason why SB: 1 chose this time to reveal the truth."

"People before your time deeply relied upon gods or hopes of peace, safety, and an after-life of hell or paradise. To have been so reliant caused a sluggish twisting and turning progression and regression through the realm of life's true expectation."

"What expectation?"

"The true expectation is the exact place humans should have advanced to. There is in actuality no margin for error on where humans should have progressed to. The reason for this no-margin rule is that we truly do not know of a god of any sort to allow us to make mistakes that we cannot correct. Each human knows instinctively that they have a qualified obligation for a general known contribution."

"What do you mean by a 'general known'?"

"From the earliest times, when humans were evolving, as were all the other animals, they also had instinct. One instinct was to preserve all that was. This is because humans also came from the earth, as did rabbits or fish. These animals have many instincts such as self-preservation, and others to include general preservation by contributing to all. None of the instincts are really lost in humans. What people do not know is that their instincts have been covered."

"By our knowledge, Eddie?"

"Yes, but during this time also, the knowledge is extremely lacking, better said, dangerously incomplete. People are advanced above the other animals, but only a hand's throw away. Humans have not been around long enough during the twentieth century to solve the problems of advanced technology. Even the inventors of the supertech are far behind harnessing the end results, which is destruction. Humans evolved slowly over a vast expanse of time. Suddenly, over a period of seventy years, which is less than one hundredth of a percent of total human existence, people discovered the explosive field of true science, which did *not* increase the general mental ability to cope with the rapid technical data now being faced. This has caused a matrix of behaviors in humans.

"Some blow off the technology and religions as well and live casual lives, consuming what they can; these are mostly the younger people but certainly not a majority of them. With these people, the instinct of general contribution is not only covered, but reversed to take away and damage. We of the future have proven that your technology, as it is, frightens children, some much more than others. These children must be recognized and counciled at the first sign of being threatened. These threats or fears come from their naturally evolved instincts that high tech is replacing them. They cannot subconsciously accept this; they cover it up due to their lack of knowledge and become involuntarily noncontributory.

"One of animals' instincts is to die if they cannot wholesomely survive or wholesomely contribute. The teenager is dying. The teenager is not the only ones failing, all age groups of all peoples are experiencing the same phenomena. The ones who are somewhat coping have a special place in the matrix. These are the people who, by genetic lines, have evolved a very short distance further mentally, and have partially escaped the instinct of general contribution to a semi-awareness of love and caring for fellow human beings, with the added strength to mentally accept the advancing sciences. Still others who have been either well educated or self-learned to accept change show much promise to help and contribute.

"The ones we are looking to are the people labeled hippies, longhairs, or organics. These select few reject high tech and go for the naturalist view; yet, they do accept high intelligence and advancement, including some high tech products and devices as computers. These people are, in fact, the only ones moving in the *best* direction of all. Some peoples, such as the Navaho Indians, are nondamaging and contributory to the planet Earth itself but not to the level of contribution of human advancement. These are good and wholesome people. The problem here is that

Earth would eventually die from our solar window. We would not have attained the technical level to accomplish eternal life.''

"But, Eddie, you say we are not to reject another's belief in God or gods.''

"Yes, we do not reject the Navahos' sacred beliefs. We just know humans did in fact reach eternal life by high technology. If their gods exist, we do not know about it, is all we are saying. We all accept the Navaho with deep respect, as we do all peoples.

"The white man is the primary blame. The Navaho were pushed into a system of existence. The rest of it is the sacrament of 'don't destroy and take only as necessary.' The Navaho retain the instinct of preservation more so than any other of the human race. The general known instinct of human contribution has been injured by the American government. It is limping and cannot function. The American government operated and made policy from belief in Jesus Christ. One god ruling another by humans.''

"Is religion instinct or made, Eddie?''

"I will prove to you, personally, that even you will invent a god, Karl. I will do this at a later time. It isn't a hard question or a puzzling dilemma of why there are so many gods. It is a simple answer. In early times of humans' awareness, the peoples were separated by what they would call vast distances. There of course was noncommunication; each society created their own beliefs. This is not a noncontributory trait specifically, but when humans used their gods, it became ultimately hindering of the should be. Humans say we have Isis and all the others, this can be acceptable if they stay put. But the natural dilemma of human weakness arises, 'my god is the only god; yours is not real,' and vice versa.

"To say it is alone hindering, deeply hindering, but to kill a god by people's physical acts of war on other people is by far worse, since it reinforces the belief in the victorious god who by all means truly may not exist. If something does not exist and we follow it, we will also fall into nonexistence. The people of the future calculated their existence eternally by scientific fact, which all have come to accept over and above any delusion of hopeful thinking. All national governments today accept scientific facts. They have to; it is the truth. None completely accepts the outsiders' religions, if anything, these factions kill one another. If factions like these had not created many instances in the past, NASA would be sending out intergalactic space vessels by now and the medical field

57

would have cured all diseases and stopped the aging process by the year 1801.''

"What?''

"If the Great Library and the thinking people of Alexandria were permitted to continue their research, you would have not needed the people of the future to save you; you would already be saved!''

"What and where was this place, Alexandria?''

"This is not important for you now, Karl. Just know that if it wasn't for religion, you would never have felt pain. You would be so advanced now that there could be no concern for the future of humanity. It would be clear and simple paradise yet still advancing. SB: 1 would have come about in the year 1984. The people were afraid *then* as they are now, but they couldn't destroy Earth. Now your people can, and are.''

"Is it just religion of each race that causes all this depression?''

"Not at all. It is speculation that does.''

"I think I'm really starting to understand why we fail. Speculation is not fact. I speculate all the time and has caused very embarrassing moments for me. Eddie, tell me, generally, what has happened to us?''

"As a mother gives birth to her child and nurtures it unto release, it is reckonable as the human plight. Earth is the mother; from out of her ground came everything. Humans evolved from lower life forms. In these very early times, Mother Earth *physically* pushed and forced our ancestors through existence. There was no choice as how we were to be other than in conformity with our environment. We were nudged and driven up to a specific point, which was where we came out of the black into a crude form of awareness, the point where we could think for ourselves in a unique manner, other than in terms of hunting for food and eating to stay alive.

"Mother Earth unintentionally gave us a 'sense' from the gene pool of advancing habitat. In the very beginning of this 'sense,' we awakened extremely fast. This is the reason the dawn of civilized man seems so abrupt and timely to your modern-day scientists. The fact that certain advanced records all over the earth popped up just a few thousand years ago is actually surprising to most. Because of this fast wake-up, we no longer could be nudged, forced, or pushed through existence. You, now, are twisting, turning yourselves through it all.

"Life now has suddenly become a squirm, a self-squirming forward in the minds of all, and all through life, you grab and pull and yank in all directions. Evolving mother earth now has no say as to your behavior.

You now control the behavior of your mother. This is the unleashment of the unknowledgeable, for you know next to nothing of what you actually do perform. Mother Earth, as well as the rest of the cosmos, does make terrible and untimely errors that are destructive. It is up to you now to use this sense to stop the destruction at its source, the unique mind of humankind.''

"What is this sense? I mean specifically."

"In the future, the completely refined and perfected sense is called 'cumulative cognition.' The meaning of cognition at this time is being capable of performing all things from your own *ideas* rather than that from somewhere else. Cumulative here means progressing to all that is within the cosmos. In other words acting out your ideas from knowing all of the quantum mechanics as well as the social/psychological information available, and the information must be collective knowledge to be undamaging.''

"I know for certain that we in 1990 are not capable of reasoning like this, more or less having all this collective information. It seems contrary to what you are saying about a future existence if we could fail and destroy ourselves."

"SB: 1 and the council know all things now. They have to prove to the entire human race that this destruction must never be allowed again by experimentation with the humans themselves. In the future, before the Blue Spot is finally assembled, humans will go on many ventures. One venture will be for each human to create a earthlike world and to populate it with creative mental beings. The mistakes made on earth can never be repeated. Here, now on earth, this twentieth-century peoples are being deliberately tested by fully unleashing them without the knowledge they need to turn into perfect beings. It is the hope for our own credibility as descendants that our ancestors can pass this near hopeless test. The Armageddon of the current future, which I will explain later, can be avoided quite easily.''

"How?"

"If you can put down the social and psychological aspects of desire and delusion and accept the hard facts."

"What facts."

"Polluting the earth for a start and then education for thirty-five percent of peoples at the four-year college level with an emphasis on science, specifically biology and the workings of the earth's ecological systems. These people could convince the other two-thirds to seek what they know and stop the destruction.''

"This is so cut and specific, Eddie. The way I see it, our twisting and turning causes the destruction.''

"Someday, Karl, your humanity, not SB: 1's or mine, yours, your humanity shall exceed your technology, shall exceed all destruction; it is in you, deep in you even now. Everyone knows this. Keep turning, the Blue Spot is in you all.''

"It is in me, Eddie, but it's so hard to pull out of me.''

"Keep turning, Karl, the others will see the truth in you.''

4

The Ultimate Test

Eddie took Karl to the future because Karl was thinking about what the people were like just before the supernova vaporized Earth. Eddie told him that Karl's train of thought was as it was hoped for, that Karl truthfully desired to learn. Karl's desire to know these people came from wondering how they lived as opposed to the ones who were being tutored by the manufactured wise men of SB: 1. It seemed to Karl that these people, being at the height of human endeavor, should be the ones doing the tutoring if anyone should. However, what he found out about people of this time is that they knew everything about themselves but very little of twentieth century humans.

Upon arriving in what was New Orleans, but 25,000 years forward, Karl could not collect what he was seeing. Eddie told Karl that he would allow Karl to see in detail within half an hour. Karl must first see things as they are from an overview and be brought into the time they were in at a graduating pace to better gain understanding.

Eddie took Karl from the city. They arrived at a country setting, where there were no people to be found. Karl noticed a river with many fish swimming upstream, wild animals and birds were throughout the area, and plant life was abundant.

"What is this place, and why are we here?"

"This is part of my curiosity for the future human beings. This is the *Hudson River.*"

Then he took Karl up high over the land to see that there were no highways from city to city. Only the places where humans dwelled were there roads. They saw that there was no pollution whatsoever; the land was virgin. Eddie told Karl that no humans are allowed to enter the expanses of land in the form of flesh or with anything man-made. To travel from city to city was done by molecular transportation. These areas could be seen and briefly visited by this means of travel only. The entire earth had been restored to a normal pace of evolution without the current interfaces of people.

Eddie, knowing Karl's thoughts, spoke to him.

"Karl, you asked a question earlier about another unseen God."

"Yes, Eddie, I tend to believe this still."

Eddie takes Karl several hundred years forward. The earth is the same, and his impression of the people is the same. The difference came in the brightness of the light on the earth. Eddie moved forward through time while observing the earth. Slowly the earth became much warmer and brighter. They saw a star becoming very bright. The people of earth cried out to God in extreme desperation. Then suddenly a massive flash moved quickly over the earth, vaporizing every living creature, plant, and animal, leaving the Earth blackened and dead.

"This actually did happen, Karl. The Earth was left void and remained void for eternity."

"You told me SB: 1 saved the planet."

"He saved everything, Karl. The council's decision was to let this happen as a measure of truth."

"A measure of truth?"

"What is your immediate feelings towards all these people dying and the waste of a perfect planet."

"I feel that if there was a God, this would not have happened."

"Maybe so, Karl. However, SB: 1 reversed the effects by time travel as you should have understood. SB: 1 observed the destruction of earth along with many humans. By another time matrix designed by SB: 1, the people of earth in this time were made unaware of SB: 1 on a worldwide experiment and invitation to an almighty God to intervene. SB: 1 let millions of years pass while exploring the universe. Then he returned to save the people of earth, even before your time, from the beginning of aware humans.

"If this unseen God exists, he chose not to intervene knowing we would save ourselves by the creation of SB: 1, and allow millions of years to pass while SB: 1 explored the universe. Then SB: 1 returned to save the people of Earth, even prior to your time, from the beginning of aware humans. The knowledge we finally possess tells us everything about our universe. Through time travel forward or past, we know there was no beginning act of creation by a God. Why would this God hide from us if he exists, why would we be allowed to gain total control and eternal existence on our own and become gods ourselves?"

"I do not know, Eddie."

"This is okay, for it is not considered negative should you choose to believe in a different unseen God. You may believe what you will, and you will live forever. You must believe in this human race, and you must believe in yourself to live eternally."

Karl looked back to the charred earth and felt deeply sorry thinking that all this creation happened by statistical chance rather than the handiwork of God. His human instinct became strong within himself with these thoughts and one basic feeling, make the best of it, make the best of life. That is what we have always looked for, even in creating our own God, to think that God is from the future and not the past is indicative of positive living from our descendants.

"Karl, you have been led to believe that life's events were meant to be, I can understand your feelings of distress. Certainly you can believe that this catastrophic event was not meant to be. A God that could create this universe as complicated and vast, should be able to forsee the supernova's effects. If time is to continue in the universe, these and other events shall occur as such as what has happened in the past. There are many hard facts humans wish and do choose to ignore based on other facts they let override their fears. You knew your Sun had a solar window of at least four billion years, but you chose to dismiss the real truth that many surrounding stars definitely have much shorter lives and will go supernova many times in the next 50,000 years. Real life is filled with real truths, why do you choose to ignore them?"

"We refuse to accept that which is without faith, or God, we use God as a crutch to say, 'yeah it's all going to end, but God will save us from our bullshit of destroying ourselves,' that is why we will fail."

"So true, and this is truly going to be the failure of your kind, your excuse to destroy!"

Karl looks around, feeling alien to Earth, he could not think this selfish way any further.

"There are many facts which are so obvious to people of your time yet not only does the average person ignore them, but the most elect chose to hide them from you. Do you know why, Karl?"

"Yes, I certainly do. They know it's going to happen, and can't do anything about it except capitalize on it for financial gain, thinking only of themselves. I do like my people though, Eddie. They are just naive about what a cool life they could live if they were forthcoming. For what I am and what my people are I can live with them, they are for the most part receptive if the facts are given them openly. For me to mingle with these future genetic have-to-be's is a horrible option especially when I think that it is our blame for their zero option existence. I am assuming that these future people are the way they are due to what we and our close descendants have done to the Earth, but if you would be so kind to clear that up I could accept them somewhat better.''

Just by Karl's outward expression, Eddie knew he was thinking that these people were very ugly and totally repulsive sexually. Karl told him he does not discount these people for their humanness of intellect, but why their unattractive appearance?

Eddie told Karl that these people had to involuntarily mutate genetically to survive the pollution years. From that time forward antiaging genetics was discovered; the only way someone died was by an unseen mishap. Consequently, there was no guideline as to who dies and who lives. The population grew in great numbers before new birth was abolished. With the great population, food supply was the main priority; the smaller ugly being you see was the only known solution. This body survives on just about anything edible, as this race can manufacture its own nutrients within the body rather than obtain vitamins and minerals from an outside source. This body can survive on the grass in your yard, just as a cow or sheep.

Karl was quiet and just observed them for some time. Their eyes were very large and compound, like an insect's—no blinking action from a noticeable eyelid, a very small nose, just vestigial ears, and a very small mouth. The skin was colorless, ghostly white, with a synthetic, durable looking texture. The main body was about one and one-half feet long with two-foot legs and one and one-half foot arms, all very skinny. The fingers were very long, nearly eight inches, including the thumb. The head was angular and longer, and together with the compound eyes, these people looked frightening. When they smiled, you felt a real sense of friendliness. Karl realized that they could not see him as he descended to ground level.

''Why do they not see us, Eddie?''

''We are oscillating, Karl. Should they see you, they would panic.''

''What do you mean?''

''These people are unaware of time travel, Karl.''

''That means an awful lot, Eddie. These people are heading for earth's destruction, aren't they?''

"Yes, they have not died yet as we are here now. Look to the north sky, Karl, and tell me what you see."

"I see a star. It is the beginning of the supernova!"

"Yes, Karl."

"I don't feel sorry for them, Eddie. I feel good about these people."

"Why, Karl?"

"Because they are the ones who directly created SB: 1 and saved themselves."

"You are saying that these people are the ones deserving of reward for their accomplishment more than people of your time, Karl."

"Yes, I am."

"You are right; however, your people contributed by surviving, generation to generation, and that is enough to warrant appreciation and a reward of eternal life."

"We all have meant well and contributed, haven't we, Eddie?"

"Karl, look to your right. What do you see?"

"A portal, like the one you came out of in the desert where I met you."

Eddie asked Karl to look into the portal.

"What do you see, Karl?"

"A hammer, like a sledgehammer, constantly bearing an immense metal wall with great intensity."

"Tell me what else you see, Karl."

"The hammer is slowly moving the wall. I can tell that with every impact, the wall moves forward. The wall has many large concave areas in it where the hammer has made impact, but the wall remains perfectly straight up and down, only moving across a smooth plain. I cannot see what is on the other side of the wall, but each time the wall moves something from the other side comes into view."

"How does it come into view, Karl?"

"Mentally, not physically."

"Do you know what this vision of the wall and hammer mean, Karl?"

"I think so, I believe this is the intense effort of humankind to move forward in life."

"You are correct, but what is the hammer?"

"You have to move the wall somehow."

"Yes, Karl, and this is your own vision and that of the people of your time as well. The portal contained no vision of its own. These thoughts of the wall and the hammer are your own. Seeing the progress of man at this time triggered your way of visualizing, your way of thinking. People of your time slammed at the wall of knowledge causing damage to the wall, which is only the people themselves; nevertheless the end result was success. The people of this time are not destructive in their advances. Look back to the people, Karl, use all that you are to perceive them.''

Karl knew Eddie did not think that all he saw was outward physical makeup of these people. The appearance of their bodies was so shocking because they were the human race, our descendants. They were obviously far advanced from twentieth-century thinking. The general appearance concerning clothing was a dead giveaway that there is no concern for fashion or vanity. Some of the people wore no clothing. None had the high fashion sense involved in trying to impress others with their looks. This not only applied to clothing, but physical appearance as well. Some of these people were very unattractive as are people today, yet they were equally treated and accepted. Eddie and Karl roamed the city for about two hours due to Karl's curiosity.

The date was May 24, 25456. They saw historical markers, which fascinated Karl. It was clear that the Japanese held the world government. The national flag had changed, yet there still remained remnants here and there of the Japanese ideographs. Even though this was the case, the rule was not a dictatorship, living was more comfortable than in the 1980s. The best way to describe Karl's feelings toward these people is that humankind finally came to its senses. Everyone was mature, and everyone was intellectual, with humor mixed in. They laughed outwardly. More than words were uttered. Karl soon realized that they were all telepathic. He saw so many people paired up face to face just smiling at each other not to deduce telepathic communication. There were no accidents, no pain, or anything negative. There were no children. Eddie told Karl that very few children were in the population as these people did not age. Each person was eternal, without the need for reproduction. The earth was indeed a big happy family in perfect harmony. To continue reproduction was a misnomer; the giving of birth was called production, since no one died, and production would be devastating without restraint.

In the two hours they walked about, Karl kept in his thoughts Eddie's comments on these people's way of thinking. He was offended by Eddie's remark about his destructive way of thinking. As time passed, Karl realized how right Eddie was. These people were highly productive in a step-by-step basis for the most part, sometimes exponential. Whichever way they accomplished or made new discoveries, patience was truly a virtue. No one was able to carelessly reach a new level of knowledge, simply due to total awareness, and that meant patience. Even with the foreseeable supernova's destructive force, people were calm and carefully sought a solution.

Eddie reminded Karl that these people did solve the problem by Superbeing One's creation. SB: 1 however altered this time as well as removing himself and all other superbeings in a matrix far above even these people's understanding, which detracted the thoughts of creating a being to save themselves. The thoughts were given to them in a way as to save themselves directly by making shelters underground and solar deflectors in space, all of which would fail due to the underestimated intensity of the supernova. SB: 1 was created in the first time line from natural human curiosity of complete collective knowledge past-present to better mankind by giving more knowledge back to mankind. The people who started work on SB: 1 had no knowledge of the supernova or even any concern for Earth's peril as they assumed Earth was safe, especially after the restoration of the environment.

The people of New Orleans, that they were observing, had no knowledge of SB: 1. They looked to themselves both individually and collectively as did people everywhere.

Without a belief in an outside power or God, they were unselfish. Their knowledge allowed them to surpass crime. There were no police. There was no military. The Japanese government faded, as intelligence now ruled, and this intelligence was more love for one another than anything else anywhere could gather. Each person was truly free. One circumstance that probably allowed this was the absence of money. People did their part to keep the earth wholesome, and each person received equal treatment and luxuries. Each lived more luxurious than any of us today, simply by the advances in technology. The technology was astounding regarding home living. Molecular science allowed for large spaces in which to live. Homes could be enlarged simply by molecular machines that would take voice commands. These homes would last forever, as the molecular devices would renew the home at the atomic level as needed. Today we would probably call this molecular recycling. A home could be reduced in size to transport, as the people shared property sites such as the beach. All the people's belongings could stay in the house while being reduced or enlarged. Sometimes the homes were moved by molecular transformers.

The vehicles had no emissions, they traveled on streets of much higher quality than that of today. Not only were these people telepathic, but they had psychic, supernatural, powers that could push and steer the vehicles, and at greater speeds than our fastest sports cars of today. When Karl noticed this, Eddie told him that this was how he caused Terrestrial Wind to move through physical space, aided by the pearlescent blue metal band he had placed around his head. The only propulsion system Terrestrial Wind had was time displacement and a small backup drive system in case of personal injury.

Karl was surprised he had waited to tell him this, as Terrestrial Wind was responding to him in thought. Karl had assumed the craft was acknowledging orders to its propulsion system. Eddie made it clear that he did not have this power, rather the molecular makeup of the head band was the source of power from his thoughts. Eddie told Karl the technology of this day could duplicate the powers of the living into the nonliving by complicated mathematical molecular arrangements, *such as the head band.* Then he reinformed Karl that he was an example of this himself. He could take on any form. He could even become the very headband Karl was wearing, or another one. This knowledge began to frighten Karl, but he knew Eddie was planning his awareness at a pace he could accept.

Eddie changed his body makeup to a silver metal ball about one inch in diameter suspended two feet before Karl's face. He continued to speak to him as he always had, audibly loud and clear. He told Karl to put out his hand. He did and the metal ball lay in his palm.

"Here I am, Karl. Make a fist and throw me into the Mississippi River."

Karl felt uplifted, and threw him as hard as he could, watching the silver ball fly away. It pulled Karl up behind it with a great sweeping force. He saw Eddie in his normal form standing far out in front of him smiling as he sped towards him. Karl landed next to him, exhilarated!

"What was that?!"

"We traveled to Los Angeles, Karl!"

"How?"

"By molecular transference, how else?"

"That is better than a ride at the fair any day! Eddie, is it always so?"

"It is just adrenaline, Karl. You'll get used to it. There are by far more exciting amusements than this for you to discover, even on your own. Do you still want to do drugs, Karl?"

"Don't fool with me now, Eddie!"

"You enjoyed the trip, I can tell, Karl. Just wait until you become a spirit!"

5

Pastime Diversion

"What are you looking at, Karl?"

"The land, if this is Los Angeles, my name is Magic Johnson."

"What looks different to you, Karl?"

"The buildings, of course, look exactly like the ones in New Orleans, but I know the Los Angeles area well, I don't see Beverly Hills and the beach front is totally wrong. The beach should curve inland from the north. This beach protrudes far out to sea."

"You are right, Karl, and it is due to the San Andreas fault line. Several miles of the western coastline settled into the sea due to several high level earthquakes."

"Yes, they said this would happen."

Eddie looked at Karl as if that generation was still his generation and he was going back to 1990, whether he liked it or not.

"What do you see on the beach, Karl?"

"My God, they are still doing it, surfing it up! Nothing really changes, well they look awfully funny though."

"I am sure they would say the same of you, Karl."

"I am sure would, I can't surf. Wait a minute. These guys are just too good!"

"What do you mean?"

"Eddie, there are hundreds of suffers out there, all riding on the same waves and not one of them has taken a dive. That's screwy. They are too close to each other, and it sure appears that they aren't balancing at all, just standing on the boards."

"That is an easy observation, Karl. The boards are doing all the work."

"Oh, don't tell me, some high tech surfboard named Flipper rides the big, or should I say, little, kahuna."

"Ha! Great, Karl, but that is basically the idea."

"Why?"

This is just a form of leisure. No one competes anymore. All have reached a physical similarity, everyone can surf and play football equally well."

"So what's the point?"

"Amusement, and some people do fall off on a swell or other water movement. You should hear the cackling laughter."

"Would the person who fell off be offended or embarrassed?"

"No, he would laugh the loudest. There are still some competitive sports, Karl, but they are not meant to be won or lost."

"Tell me of these sports."

"You've played tennis, Karl. Would you like to view this sport?"

"For a while, I suppose. But if we go, let's go by the method you've been using, not this molecular transformer."

"Okay, Karl."

They are again instantly transported. This time, Eddie shows Karl a tennis match.

"There is competition here, Karl. These people playing are friends. Can you tell me what you see different about the way the game is being played?"

"These little people are a lot faster, and they never seem to miss a shot!"

"Yes, they don't play sets or matches, they play until the shot is missed, and if they wish, they will continue to play. How do you think they can play so well?"

"You said they all have reached similarity, and could play sports equally."

"That is true, Karl, do you think that is totally physical?"

"They are using telepathy here, right?"

"Yes."

"So they probably know where the ball is going to be all the time, don't they?"

"It can get much deeper than that, Karl, the competition here among friends is the most intense and, at the same time, more trusting than anyone of your time could allow. The game has become personal, Karl, and is more than a game; it is a thrill! Can you let your imagination wander on this, to carry over other aspects of these people?"

"Mmm, yes! Sex must be great!"

71

"Karl, you are exacting. The point is that these people interact in everything they do very well, not just sports."

"I know, Eddie, but I have to be honest, I really want to know about their sex life."

"The point in human interaction is beyond the current level of success during your time."

"They probably do interact well in general with this added ability. I think that sex would be their ultimate use of this ability."

"You're very wrong about that, Karl. The ultimate use of this ability goes toward furthering mankind's advances for better living, but sex is a major part of that too."

"Might I say that ultimate use was a bad choice of words. I'll bet this telepathic ability makes them enjoy sex more, intensely more."

"I have to say, Karl, your persistent, but right, so what really has your curiosity?"

"I'd have to say it's twofold curiosity."

"Tell me, Karl."

"Well, I'm a much lower life form, right?"

"Yes, you are."

"So that would mean I couldn't have sex the way these people do, even if I had one of my own kind, right?"

"You mean if you were suddenly telepathic, Karl?"

"Yes."

"Well, if what you're driving at is something you wish to do, that is possible with the head band, and another female of your kind equally equipped."

"Oh, no! Eddie, that's fine."

"Well, would you just like me to elaborate on the sex life of these people?"

"Enlighten me, Eddie."

"Sex is twofold with these people, Karl. Is this where your meaning of a twofold question originates."

"No, Eddie. I was playing around with you. I was trying to be psychologically interested in their sex lives, since I didn't think you'd discuss it with me. I was going to say you should tell me about their sex lives, as it should be the most trusting use of telepathy. With that in mind, honesty and trust is what these people have completely delved into."

"I believe I understand you, Karl. By revealing their sex life to you, you would be grasping at these people's highest order of living due to their trust in one another. Even if I could show this to you, you could not comprehend it.''

"I already knew that.''

"So what was the second part of your pretentious question, Karl?''

"I just wanted to know if they had sex and, if so, how often. For all I know they may think of sex as being crude and basic, being so advanced as these people are.''

"Karl, all you had to do was ask me.''

"Well, Eddie, I—''

"I know, Karl. Many people of your time are still very bashful and sex shy.''

"Hmmm, people of this time are not?''

"They don't have to be bashful, Karl! They are fully aware. You've coined 'so advanced,' they may not think of something so basic as sex. I must tell you the situation is quite the contrary. They have become further advanced since they've continued to practice sex. Knowing this, do you think that they should be bashful or sex shy?''

"Like I said, Eddie, enlighten me!''

"There is reproductive sex, and totally separate from this, there is a complete exchange of human being sexuality. Which would you like to know?''

"This sounds way out and beyond. I've convinced myself that I really want to know all that I can of these people.''

"For the most part, Karl, I've already told you mostly everything that you can comprehend concerning their way of thinking. Concerning sex, normal physical sex as you engage in, is marginally the same as reproductive sex. If two people really love each other in your time, sex can be very beautiful and romantic. The same is true here. They always engage in sexual arousement and lengthy foreplay. During the rare reproduction, telepathy is outwardly discarded concerning one's own identity and is directed towards the creation of new life. This telepathy is used minimally so as not to interfere with the unborn child. Love between the mates during physical intercourse is mostly the center of this sexual behavior. But because of what they are, telepathy remains in this part of life. You have to understand telepathy better in its normal form to appreciate this addition to sex. I can make you understand better by one of the negative aspects of having sex in your time without telepathy.''

"What is that, Eddie?''

"You have been emotionally turned off by a talkative or inattentive sex partner, and because they do not know your desires. Outward speaking such as saying would you please be quiet or please don't do that, makes matters worse. This is true not only because of the inability to make your partner understand but also the physical quality of verbal communication."

"I'm not sure I understand what you mean about physical quality, Eddie."

"Verbal communication is extremely crude, Karl. Compounded with the imperfect people who speak, many imperfections arise. People of your time have extreme difficulty with communication. They all have to speak with a tone of voice; this tone may be accidentally misused to seem, let's say, a sarcastic remark. The tone may be correct, the correct words may be used in the best of circumstances, but still, there is untoward communication just simply due to the physical roughness of verbal language. This is especially true because people of your time so often get away with a lie, many people don't believe what they hear. Rarely does communication of your time bring total satisfaction; there is almost always doubt. You've heard the expression, 'Words cannot say,' which is now the case with advanced humankind. Telepathy has improved the quality of life by far more than what you could comprehend after one thousand years of tutoring."

"I do comprehend that if people of my time were telepathic and used it with advanced knowledge, our sex lives would be great, as I first said."

"You are abusive, Karl!"

"Maybe so, Eddie, but I am just having fun with you right now."

"You wouldn't be if I hadn't stimulated your mind and body with about all the peace I can give you."

"You are still doing that, aren't you, Eddie?"

"Yes, you would be in a shock and close to death if I stopped distracting you."

"This frightens me just thinking about where I am."

"Good, Karl, so let us continue with the sexual behavior of these people. What you know of reproductive sex is all you will be able to comprehend, with the exception of near total birth control. This is a simple fact; put too many eternal beings on the planet, the planet will die, so reproductive sex is rare. Keeping that in mind, nonreproductive sex has been designed by the people for pleasure that knows no boundary.''

"They designed sex?''

"As synthetic as this sounds, with advanced awareness, it becomes more of a natural reality than the designed sex of your time.''

"Designed sex of my time?''

"Designer jeans, hair, clothing, body sculpting, oral contraceptives, Karl?''

"Well, I would say that is quite different.''

"Is it different, Karl? The designed sex of these advanced people is somewhat different than your normal sex.''

"How different?''

"For one thing, they do not have to physically touch each other.''

"So it's not really sex sex.''

"No, Karl, it is sex sex sex. It is sex and more sex. It just depends on 'your' view right now of what sex is.''

"Well, Eddie, to me sex is male-female, female-male, getting—''

"I know, Karl, I know what sex is like. Let me give you a typical two-person family example of sex. You must understand that this is oversimplified and minimized. First, telepathy is an extension of the mind. Telepathy can allow the mind to partially leave the body. Imagine fictional people, Jane and Robert. Robert is leaving for work in the morning. In your time, Robert would have taken a little of Jane's love with him. Robert, in this time, not only does that, but he also takes a little bit of Jane's being with him, leaving a little of his being with her. They do not just communicate as if they had radios, they *feel* each other at a distance, more so than you do at the height of your euphoric momentarily enjoyed sexual orgasm.''

"I felt Sandi more just sitting on the Owhyee Canyon edge than I ever did having sex with her.''

"Yes, Karl, and that is exactly what I am talking about. When these people are apart, they feel each other more than you can when you are together. Do you understand, Karl?''

"Yes, they are not really apart, maybe physically, but that part of them which is so much more real is together.''

"To help you understand more fully, Karl, they are not just together, they are intertwined and mixed. If you have two colors of paint, blue and yellow, and you mix them what happens?''

"I remember from art class; that would make green, Eddie.''

"This is the same as two telepathic lovers, they mix and find something together that is wonderful. The lovers indulge themselves in ecstasy far beyond your abilities. Each partner knows exactly what it is about their sexual mate from their one hundred percent knowledge of each other and how to please them from this."

"This really is far beyond my generation, Eddie. Telepathic love certainly is true love. You would know for certain if someone was pulling your chain for money or self-interest."

"Yes, in your time, telepathy would be devastating to many people. The good news is that your people are encroaching on a reality level allowing them to say good-bye to dishonest mates. People are in fact using hidden misunderstood powers to find new love. This is one reason why divorce is so high. The 1980s and 1990s are truly the beginning of the breakthrough years in mental awareness. Hate will be stronger, and love will be less common yet many times more powerful than all the hate of this time."

Karl often wondered about the future of his generation.

"I shall show you every detail of your future generation, Karl, but first, you must take with you the fundamental understanding of these future people to help you show your people the peace that is humanly attainable, not the pending destruction waiting for you."

"You're saying my generation will be destroyed."

"Karl, what do you already know of the final destruction of these future people we now observe?"

"I know that the supernova will completely destroy the earth, yet SB: 1 comes back and saves them."

"Who is SB: 1, Karl. Ultimately, who is SB: 1?"

"SB: 1 is all the people's knowledge combined. SB: 1 is the people."

"So who saved these people, Karl?"

"The people, ultimately."

"Yes, and just as the people of your time can destroy themselves, they can save themselves. Put these things aside momentarily as we continue to observe our future and the leisure they pursue."

"Why do they pursue leisure so earnestly, Eddie?"

"They have reached physical and mental perfection, Karl. They have not reached the spiritual realm, which is eternal in life as well as new discovery. They are not even sure spirituality exists; therefore, in the perfection they live, they seek paradise. They have reached the mental, honest awareness of knowledge that cannot allow a falsehood. This allows the total mixing of the mind during sex, which is the climax of human trust, for many obvious reasons, not to mention that a sexual partner's desires shall be known for eternity.''

"That makes me wonder if they have more than one sexual partner.''

"What does your knowledge and awareness of these people cause you to believe, Karl?''

"I would have to say they only have one sexual relationship through eternity.''

"From your way of thinking, Karl, to where they are now took over twenty thousand years. You are correct, they could never leave the one they love and have sex with another. These thoughts alone make you feel as if you are maturing towards a better and advanced life, do they not, Karl?''

"I want to be perfect, Eddie, everyone does, we just know it is so far off.''

"Not true, Karl. You are closer than you believe, especially if you try.''

"I think people of my time have quit trying.''

"As I said, hate will abound, but there shall be the loving, which is stronger and can stop the destruction.''

"These people discovered eternal life, Eddie. They had time to work on perfection.''

"They had more than time, Karl, they had the current way of thinking from a proper culture. Think, Karl, they could have destroyed themselves in time as well.''

"Yes, I see your point. So what was their way of thinking or proper culture?''

"The world was in the same general line of thought even though it took a world war to do so. Many had tried to do this in the past. Alexander the Great tried, Genghis Khan tried, the Romans tried, and Hitler tried, but they all failed. It took a nation of humility and dignity, a people who originally believed in themselves and the planet; they had no god. In their homeland, they served each other with great esteem and the highest of moral values for each other. They made their land beautiful and productive. These were truly the most artistic people of all time past. Do you know who these people were, Karl?''

"You told me in the first line of time, in the natural order of life, world rule came to be under the Japanese.''

"You understand, Karl?"

"Yes, so these people living in luxury are the result of Japanese thinking?"

"Not ultimately, just as I am distracting your anxiety and giving you peace, SB: 1 is giving these people peace. SB: 1 is distracting them from creating a solution to the supernova's destructive force. The council of the first time line came to agreeement that the supernova should be allowed to destroy the earth, leaving only SB: 1 behind."

"The council is all the people who gained eternal life in the first time line, correct, Eddie?"

"Yes."

"So what happened to them? I thought they went to be tutored and become spiritual and enter Heaven and create their own universe. I saw the city of God, Eddie."

"What you saw does exist now. SB: 1 simply traveled back in time before his creation and began distracting the people who would have created the would-be SB: 1."

"What about the council? If they were seeking a solution to an a unseen power or god, simply letting the earth self-destruct would be foolish. No intelligent god would reveal himself for this reason, since he had not already done so!"

"SB: 1 was given a solution to this problem by the council, Karl."

"What solution?"

"SB: 1 killed the council, the entire human race became void. SB: 1 returned to Earth 500 years before the people created the supercomputer, which was SB: 1."

"He killed everyone?"

"It was the only solution, Karl. They really had a desire for the unknown." Karl cannot see this as perfect thinking. "Karl, it was the only solution. It came down to a process of elimination concerning solving the *problem of SB: 1 or God.* As you witnessed, SB: 1 blends into all the people in the end. After seeing all of the council's concern of having designed SB: 1, SB: 1 could not be their god. In SB: 1's feelings received from creation by man. SB: 1 gave everything back to man by giving the spirit to man after man's tutorial perfection. The spirit was SB: 1; SB: 1 is no more; man becomes spirit; the spirit is complete and perfect."

"This is heartbreaking, Eddie."

"No, Karl, when you receive the spirit, you will be comforted. You will understand from beginning to end as the spirit is, and is now, and shall ever be man eternal."

"We are truly alone."

"You are truly gods, Karl. You are the beginning of life. Have faith in yourself and the human race! Karl, I know what you desire the most. Tell me what you now feel!"

"Freedom, Eddie!"

"Yes! Too free to think some tyrannical god rules your life! You rule your life now. From the day you are born you can do this! Now that you have become aware you can be a free person. This has always been who you really are."

"I know. That is why I had my own business and was a slave only to myself, went where I wanted, with no one telling me what not to do. This is why I committed crimes. I truly do know better now, Eddie. I really can see why these future people enjoy life to the fullest extent; there is nothing to be guilty of or wrong about having fun."

"Karl, this is a good time to continue the observation of these people, as I cannot allow you to dwell on the seriousness of the human flight; it is damaging as well as good to someone of your youth. You have seen and experienced enough seriousness for now. Relax, come and see the fish under the surfers."

"What fish? These are people playing games underwater?"

"What game do they play?"

"Looks like tag to me. One person is trying to touch one of the thousands that are under here! They move faster than I can run on dry land!"

"This is a great skill, Karl. It is the thinking of one against thousands, and in the thousands, one is pinpointed upon a physical point in space by a telepathic misjudgment to get tagged. It is how fast one can change his mind without himself knowing where he will go next, giving only a thought's notice to his hopeful victim of the tag."

"They move like schools of fish away from the person who has been tagged 'it'."

"They feel the resistance of the water as you do, Karl. They just think their way through it at speeds faster than any fish can swim."

"They do not seem to be coming up for air."

"Oh, I haven't told you; these people do not have to breath anymore. It is a carryover from the pollution years, genetic engineering."

"Eddie, you've said that these people can be surprised—the example of falling off a surfboard. This tells me that they could in fact have serious accidents causing death."

"This is true, they do have accidental deaths. If someone is killed by accident, it is of minor concern, since they can be brought back to life by molecular rejuvenation. The doctor of this time is a molecular transformer. Each person's complete biological makeup is recorded and stored mathematically in computers. When there is an injury, death, or sickness, the body is placed in a molecular transformer and transported through space while the computer arranges and rearranges the body at molecular levels to one hundred percent original specifications. Just as your body was cleansed of the human immune deficiency virus, this process heals the body from physical injury as well."

"I understand. It feels good to know I'm in the proper order that I should be, Eddie. Nice to know there is a perfect doctor."

'That's what these people call it, as funny as this may seem to you."

"They call it the doctor?"

"Yes."

"That is humorous to me."

"Whoever said they didn't have humor?"

"All I have seen is nothing but fun and games. Of all things, a mechanical doctor. I'll bet they don't have lawyers anymore."

"No, they were all put out of work."

"Huh, no lawyers no doctors."

"Kind of takes the worry out of dying, wouldn't you agree, Karl?"

"If this machine existed during my time, woe, we'd have some serious dementia. Can you imagine, Eddie?"

"Karl, you are really a pill. I do understand though, and thanks be to the uniform progress of technology and higher order of thinking, this has never been a concern. There is in fact a sense of immortality in these people that carries over to a more daring recreational life. Would you like to see a recreational park that is somewhat comparable to a state fair in your time, Karl?"

"This has got to be entertaining, Eddie. Karl was completely fascinated with Marriott's Great America Amusement Park in California. An amusement park 27,000 years into my future. You think I would say no, I don't want to go, Eddie!"

"It is the place where most accidents occur, Karl."

"We are oscillating in time, they can't see me, and I don't have to participate, so what would be the concern?"

"They push themselves to their physical and telepathic limits for research, Karl. The way of thinking stretches a bit farther than you may be able to grasp. The visit may be sickening to you. In their humor there is extreme seriousness as well.''

"Research?''

"Karl, you are intrigued with the abilities of your modern-day athletes, such as the Washington Husky football team. You are surprised to see how well they play this game, aren't you?''

"You bet, they ripped the Sooners in the 1984 Orange Bowl. I wished they could have played Brigham Young that year, I'd of wagered big bucks on the Huskies.''

"They will get their chance, Karl, if both teams wish, but let's stick to the research here. The football players pitted themselves against each other with an all out desire to win, right?''

"Of course, Eddie.''

"They did so to win and, whether intentionally or inadvertently, they improved their abilities. So do these people of the future, they push themselves to become better.''

"Well, that makes sense, Eddie, especially since they have nothing to lose. This gives me an additional insight concerning these people, too.''

"How so, Karl?''

"Even though they live a life of leisure, there is still a sense of ambition in them.''

"Most definitely, Karl, this is just a part of advanced awareness. When this much knowledge is possessed, a perfect balance becomes a natural way of life. No single person here shall regress in life, and no single person will advance above the others; their advances are equally shared. What I'd like you to know now, Karl, is how these people travel to and from a place, such as the amusement park where we are also going.''

"Eddie, if it's that transference whatever stuff, count me out.''

"Don't get jumbled, Karl. All I'm asking is that you observe.''

"Let's go.''

"You know, Karl, I may have given you a bad experience transporting to L.A. The method they use is molecular transference.''

"I don't care, Eddie, if it is bad or how they do it. I ain't going that route again and, besides, I got the rest of my life to find out—whoaa—dammit, I said no!''

"We are here, Karl. Isn't this great!''

"Eddie, if I ever am able to get even with you—''

"Look around, Karl.''

"God . . . bless! What in the hell are they doing!?''

"Having the time of their lives, Karl."

"Jesus, I can't tell people about this, no way."

"Try to be careful with your emotions, Karl, but you can reveal some of what you see here today."

"Eddie! Some of these people are killing, I mean they're trying to kill—they are killing each other. This is some kind of game that demands entering someone's territory, stealing his whatever that is, and getting the hell out alive. The course in and out is so difficult, I couldn't walk through without getting poked by those things I can't even describe. This absolutely cannot be considered fun or amusing, Eddie."

"This is but one segment of the park, Karl. Here, people are very serious in their endeavor to perfect body and mind."

"I see. They go to and beyond their limit to find errors, then correct themselves. So it must be like never knowing until you go the distance, even to death. But how do they heal themselves and come back to life so quickly? It is an instant."

"Karl, look up to the four towers at each corner of the park."

"I see what looks like satellite dishes on the top of each tower."

"Yes, they are a type of transmitter which are connected to a central storage computer. The computer is linked to the main molecular transporter. Every person's biological makeup is on record, so in the event of injury or death, they are renewed instantly, as each person is closely monitored. In essence, the entire park is a molecular transmitter. No one is in any real danger here, and since there is no fear of pain, aging, or death, people are free to excel or just have fun. This same system is in every part of the country, it is just a little more intensified here."

"So they simply pick up where they left off."

"If they learned of their mistake or found out they were attempting something that actually could be accomplished. If they know from the failed attempt that it could not be accomplished, then they stop the effort and evaluate the particular circumstance. A trial-and-error approach is accepted but secondary to a thought-out solution, usually figured by logic."

"You mean people can't just come in here and bang their way through, hoping each new attempt is successful."

"Yes, besides, this is not the way these people think anyway. Total awareness and collective knowledge doesn't permit such behavior from within each person."

"Like I said, glad this doesn't exist in my time! These people look like they have supernatural power."

"Mostly supernatural. Here, all the precognitive, psychic, and telepathic powers they possess are put to full potential. If you look carefully, you'll see that they only use body parts when psychic powers are at full peak. What might look like a person running in the maze is only due to what you expect to see."

"I do see that now. They only put their feet down in certain spots to gain traction where the maze is extremely difficult to maneuver. It makes me wonder how close they are to becoming spirit."

"That is a long distance off yet, Karl. What you see is in fact awesome, but the spirit is not even imaginable to these people. That should give you an idea of the greatness of the spirit, but I'm afraid to say you cannot grasp the idea of being infinite."

"The spirit is infinite, Eddie?"

"The spirit could be nothing less than infinite."

"To think that you're telling me this, and I am going to be a spirit someday is just total entrancement!"

"Even after becoming spirit, entrancement will still exist, Karl."

"All this is necessary to become spirit, all this madness even what they do here today?"

"Absolutely, Karl, and many more years of teaching when all is said and done on earth."

"We are all going to the school I saw outside the city of God, aren't we?"

"Yes, Karl. Come now, I have something to show you."

Eddie took him to a part of the park that is what we today would call the zoo. This portion of the park had all the animals that ever lived on Earth from the beginning. He saw dinosaurs and apes and even semi-humans who were in every stage of evolution up to modern homo sapiens, and they were alive.

"Eddie, you told me these people could not travel in time, and I know for sure these animals were extinct in any time line. How did they do this?"

"I'll give you a clue, Karl, since I know you will be able to figure this one out for yourself. They, as you know, have all the original fossils or bones of these creatures."

"They have this kind of technology to rebuild and create fleshly animals from the past?"

"Yes, this is easy to do, Karl. Think about what they can do to themselves."

"I guess so, considering the fact they can come back from death."

"It is all molecular physics, Karl. Take a bone, figure out the molecular design and build a living creature from it. The wonderful thing about it is that this is not guesswork, but it is exact and original."

"Not to mention that we've saved rare and extinct species, Eddie."

"To some extent, Karl, this was one hope to try and save mankind past at the beginning of this discovery. However they found out that the evolutionary process could only duplicate character or instinct. What you see are a bunch of stupid animals in their fleshy original design."

"Well, that's due to their being just manufactured flesh from a machine, Eddie."

"Yes, but they did think that if a person's DNA code was recovered, manufactured flesh would have duplicating effects of personality as well."

"You mean they were going to try to save people from the past using this method?"

"Yes, but you know what?"

"What, Eddie?"

"This very effort is what fed SB: 1 the necessary input to pursue time travel."

"Now you make it sound as if SB: 1 is a computer, Eddie."

"At this particular time of discovering DNA manufacture, SB: 1 was a computer, Karl."

"What brand name, Eddie?"

"Human brain, Karl."

"Speaking of humans, Eddie, I saw some of what seemed close to humans earlier. Can we see them up close?"

"Yes, Karl, but I just want to let you know that I hid the twentieth-century humans from you so you wouldn't be upset."

"You have my kind in a zoo!?"

"You're going to be surprised, Karl. Just about anybody who was anybody is here from the beginning."

"You mean prominent people from the past are here."

"Yes, Karl."

"Haven't these people heard of canvas, Eddie?"

"You mean an art gallery?"

"Uh, hmmm, yes."

"Oh, this is much better, it's realistic and entertaining."

"Oh, dear God, entertaining!?"

"Do not think this is cruel. These animals are actually content to be in existence. Remember, they are living now but were not before. Any life is better than no life if in no discomfort."

"Okay, let's have a look-see, Eddie. Animals, for crying out loud."

"Some of the people you will not recognize, as they did not exist in your time line, and others will not be here because they did not exist in this first time line, such as Moses or Christ."

"Whoa, you're telling me more than a handful here, Eddie."

"Yes, but save that thought for now. I'll show you Moses and Christ in your time line later."

Eddie led him to the area that modern day humans were kept; they were in fact caged in an environment that fitted their proper time of existence.

"Do you see anyone you recognize, Karl?"

"Yes, quite a few. That means time has been retained somewhat the same."

"That is a good definition, Karl. Who do you recognize?"

"Well, that is Albert Einstein in a physics lab, and there is the rock group known as the Beatles playing "Twist and Shout" to a mob of crazy young girls."

"Don't forget the guys too, Karl."

"Yeah, but I was never that crazy."

"That's not how I saw it, Karl—'She loves you, yeah, yeah, yeah!' "

"All right, so I got into it a bit. What's this over here?"

"Oh, you don't really need to see this part, it's just past war veterans and such."

"Oh, no, I do. That's Adolf Hitler, and over here is—"

Karl was caught looking with his peripheral vision while observing President John Kennedy to see what could cause his heart to fail. He looked straight on and away from Kennedy and became speechless.

"Karl—I wanted—"

"First I see myself dead in a jet; now I'm a living monster in a zoo being accused of mass murder, Eddie!"

"Karl, these people do not know who you really are. They just know what you did that day was catastrophic. God knows your heart."

"I sure hope so, and I hope these people will be able to accept me."

"They will, Karl, when they know your heart."

"Hell, they've got me penned up as the Baghdad Bastard walking around in there!"

"What I am about to do, is not generally accepted procedure but I have to use my power to put these people's point of view into your thinking process so you'll understand. Touch my hand, Karl."

"I do see now, Eddie. They have no idea or concept of what actually happened that day."

"And that is what will happen many times over when all people come together in peace, Karl. They shall see the hidden truths of every circumstance ever taking place on earth. Even the lies of the so-called great leaders. Many innocent people shall be cleared, Karl. Many great people shall be exposed; they will be the most difficult to teach, if at all."

"That makes me feel good, Eddie. Damn, I'll be able to prove it wasn't me who pulled down Monica's shorts in gym class!"

"You really did get punished for that one, didn't you, Karl?"

"I was trying to be funny, Eddie, hoping to forget this crap I see here."

"I know. Let's go watch a game, Karl."

"From this point on, the secrets of the future cannot be revealed to our time as their early arrival could be a detriment. Simple chemicals, for example, used in the twentieth century when mixed in exacting quantities give psychic powers if consumed. These powers are far and above what people could properly use. Any one person could gain significant control of the people."

There were many games being played, such as racing energy fields in the form of cars. They also played against robots and machines in various sporting events. The purpose was for human advancement. In our time, these same works would cause failure. In our time, we shall advance as it should be, on our own.

6

Alpha

Eddie knew that revealing the future to Karl was insignificant considering this proved nothing about a beginning or creation. Karl really did not want to tell him he needed proof, but he wanted to see creation from the beginning.

"You're becoming telepathic as a result of what you've seen, Karl. Knowledge is passed on to you easily. You have to learn tranquility and patience. The messages I am receiving from you are mixed with anxiety. I am not criticizing you, just helping you to become aware."

"I feel frustrated when I want to show something I can't, or feel I cannot ask about."

"This is true of all people during your time. You were brainwashed to not question God or creation. I will show you later that this was a misinterpretation, not given by SB: 1, but by people of your past, one of them being Moses."

"You mean Moses from the Bible?"

"Yes, Karl."

"My interest is during this time and before."

"We are drawing closer to what you want to ask me to do, Karl. Do you really want to go and see the beginning?"

"Yes, I do. I want to see how all this got started, from day one."

"We will do better than that, you shall see the beginning of the universe and before. You shall witness the billions of years which are the making of the rare planet Earth. Come and witness darkness never before seen, Karl."

"I can't even see my hand, are you there, Eddie?"

"Right next to you, Karl."

"This darkness is different."

"How is it different, Karl?"

"It's like I can see the darkness itself."

"Many people wouldn't notice this, Karl, but you are right, the darkness is visible."

"It is pure black, Eddie, no flaws, I can describe it best as clear black."

"I myself cannot orient our position of this beginning darkness. It does not make a difference if we travel billions of years further past, this is how it always was, pure darkness."

"You don't know where we are?"

"No, Karl, we shall travel forward in time to orient ourselves by a marker we shall see."

"What shall we see, Eddie?"

"A dense formation of matter that has a very crude make-up. The molecular structure of this dark matter can withstand unimaginable pressures without nuclear fission or fusion. This same matter is still abundant around the universe and possesses a threat to mankind in the future, as you shall see when we orient ourselves to the beginning marker. You will see a glowing. I will bring us closer to it when we come to the correct time, which we call Alpha. After we reach Alpha, we shall see the glow; then I shall reverse time so you can see the formation of the matter. This is Alpha, Karl. See the glow."

"It is huge, Eddie!"

"This great collection of matter is immeasurable by twentieth-century standards and numerically unthinkable."

"Why is it glowing?"

"This matter is under such gravitational pressure and is mixed with other elements that a smoldering effect has taken place. We shall travel back in time now, as we are close enough."

The glowing stopped and he could see the black matter, as Eddie had given him vision to see in the darkness. He saw the matter getting smaller and smaller from within, then vanishes into the darkness.

"Where has it gone, Eddie?"

"It collected here from the Great Dense Universe, which is in a close plain to ours but a different dimension. This is a bleed-over to ours."

"Has SB: 1 traveled to these other dimensions?"

"Yes, and only to find desolation through eternity past and future."

"So if these great universes of black matter exist without ignition, why did this one at Alpha?"

"This is the key, Karl. This matter collected in our universe, which has its own elements. These elements were spread sporadically and thinly through vast expanses of space. The black matter caused gravitational forces pulling these free elements to the matter. Not only to the black matter but deep within it, which eventually caused a tremendous explosion from the mixing of all these free elements under great pressures. Before this explosion, the black matter acted as a buffer to these elements by being an insulator. This delayed the explosion for a much longer duration. If these elements had collected on their own in isolation, the explosion would have happened much sooner.

"The matter in our universe has a density that can compress when not active much more greatly than the black matter. When the matter is active it usually will make a star if collected together in great amounts. Active and nonactive matters collected together in Alpha with the black matter bleed. When the density level reached a threshold point that the black matter could no longer mediate, our universe was born by an immense explosion. This explosion rocked all universes and dimensions. This would have killed all life if it existed. Karl, we're going to travel forward in time now to point Alpha and from there to the formation of Earth."

Karl began to see the black matter forming as if it was pouring into space from nowhere. The matter formed a long cylindrical shape, but was more round than long. After it stopped gaining in size, he could see gases and particles being drawn into it with great speed and force. As time passed, the gases and particles were drawing into the black matter at a very high rate. It looked like a large sink with water whirling down the drain. After this the process slowed so only sporadic clouds of gas were entering the black matter. Soon after this, the cylindrical ball began to glow brighter and brighter. Karl could see holes and cracks in the black matter with extremely bright rays of light shining outwards. Then in a split second, the entire mass became totally white light. Eddie told Karl to turn around.

"What do you see, Karl?"

Karl turned, looking away from the light, to see a blank universe illuminated.

"I see distance, Eddie!"

"You see eternity distance. Look around, Karl."

"I see other universes, including the one that contains the black matter. In these other universes were light, but the light of Alpha nearly darkened them. How can we see these other universes, Eddie?"

"This is Alpha, the most powerful energy ever released, it is not just light. Alpha contains elements from many universes. These elements from each universe allow for the visibility of each one's original universe; this is an attribute of physics. Look back at Alpha, Karl."

Karl turned and saw a very large corona coming from around Alpha. Then he saw great flows of bright glowing light moving outward like lava from a volcano. A second later, the entire collection of matter exploded shooting debris into every universe at great speeds. Some of the explosive matter continued to flow in streams. These streams were long and curved and eventually separated, forming blobs of light. After a while, he saw these blobs of light breaking down further into millions of lights by exploding again and again. He saw that these collections of light were forming galaxies. They raced away from Alpha, mostly in whirling lines. He looked back at Alpha and saw a much smaller round sphere remaining.

Eddie told him this was point Alpha, the remnant of the nonactive matter from our universe. He said there is no such matter anywhere else known with such density. This sphere was more than two million times the size of our sun. Alpha was more than 200,000 trillion times the size of our sun. Earth is now so far away from point Alpha that it cannot be seen or heard. There is no light at point Alpha. Point Alpha contains one seventh of the nonactive matter in our universe. The other six-sevenths are mixed in the now active stars and other parts of our universe. There is no active matter at point Alpha.

"SB: 1 has named the sphere Death, Karl, for nothing can survive here except a spirit. And there is nothing here for the spirit. But in this place called Death, life has gone out fleeting, in victory."

"Where is the life, Eddie?"

"Only on Earth, where I am taking you now. Look at Earth, Karl."

Karl saw Earth from a distance in space. The moon was revolving around our completely white-clouded world. He saw bright flashes of light through the clouds. Lightening was striking Earth constantly, and rain fell on the hot surface, which vaporized into steam. After some time passed, the rain cooled Earth and oceans and lakes formed. He saw only one land mass at the northern part of Earth. They continued to move forward in time to see the land masses separate. Then, in polar regions, ice caps formed, causing water levels to recede. Karl was able to identify the separate land masses between South America and Africa all the way up to New York and France. Eddie took him to the surface and showed him the beginnings of life. He explained to him that Earth had a diverse composition of elements from many universes. There were active molecules that had polarities, causing attraction to other molecules. He called these links.

After many millions of years, these links grew in pools of water in the moist parts of Earth. Without any life force involved, only physical properties of the elements, these links became long and abundant. When certain links were at the proper length in the proper temperature, they produced proteins. These proteins eventually coated the links. As the links survived within the protein coat, they continued to grow and break, which is a simple form of replication. These new links gained new protein coats. Eventually these links came into contact with new proteins from the changes that took place in Earth's environment. The links were then able to replicate themselves by these proteins running alongside the links. The cells were formed by this process and became the first true living material on Earth, basically a very simple germ or virus.

By this same process, bacteria and algae evolved including a non-plant cell, mostly from the germ or virus line. They developed into the single-celled animals, which by the same process of physics became more and more advanced. These properties of physics developed what is called the life force. This life force is a consciousness at the molecular level. It is not a thinking process; rather, it is a force of physics. Your immune system works this way today. With this force of physics, evolution was accelerated. Many diverse animals came into being, but only ones that could adapt to the environment it was living in.

Eddie said that they were going to move through time quickly now.

"Karl, tell me what you see."

They were high over Earth again over Utah.

"I see green plants and thick brush with marshes scattered around. This entire area is a thick, green jungle. I see insects and worms appear."

As each moment passed, the animals became more abundant and larger. Karl saw the dinosaurs and flowering plants come. There were no ice caps at this point and Earth looked warm and humid again. Clouds formed and electrical storms occurred. The larger animals died, and smaller ones ruled. There were simian life forms, which developed further and further. The climate got cooler, and then Earth was mostly an arctic planet. After this, the simians and other animals continued to advance to modern species. Karl saw people that looked heavy-boned living in shelters. There was another, but much shorter, period of arctic climate.

Mankind diminished severely during this arctic period. The more advanced and intelligent races survived. There were disputes between remaining races, leaving only the modern races that most resemble modern man.

These modern looking species were able to defeat the primitive species by intelligence rather than strength. The gap between man and ape was not crossed, and they did not dispute with one another. The world was living mostly in peace, with humans separated by geological boundaries. From this time, they continued to change, but very little as each one evolved according to their own environment. He looked at Earth and saw that the Chinese slowly evolved over millions of years, as other species in a given environment, as Eddie had explained. This evolution started at the beginning of each circumstance given. There was nothing that did not conform to this physical property. Eddie stopped the forward march in time at a point where Earth looked as it does today.

"Karl, you are 147,000 years before Christ. Here mankind has become conscious of who he is in relation to Earth and other life forms. The family life is not bonded yet; however, there is a sense of cultivation in the mind of man. Man wishes to become better here. It is here where SB: 1 gives man a soul, an eternal field in and about man that shall be resurrected by choice of the council. This soul cannot die without the consent of this council."

Eddie moved them forward again in time. Karl saw civilization progress greatly in China, then South America, and Egypt. He thought how all of this would be a theologian's nightmare—evolution or theology. Considering all that he saw, Karl was not convinced that God did not exist. God could have set things in motion by the black matter bleed, then He could have stepped back and maybe just spoke to people in the Bible here and there. He spoke these thoughts to Eddie.

"Consider some biblical writings, Karl, as opposed to what evolutionists claim. I know you have heard of the Tower of Babel."

"Yes, that is where a large tower was being built by thousands of people, and God gave them different languages."

"First, Karl, why did God give them different languages?"

"I guess because they would be capable of great achievement."

"What is wrong with that? Why would God want to hold the people down?"

"I don't know, Eddie."

"Let's start from the beginning of this particular Bible story. The verse says that now the whole earth used the same language and the same words. And it came about as they journeyed east, that they found a plain in the land of Shinar and settled there. They said to one another, Come, let us make bricks and burn them thoroughly. They used brick for stone, and they used tar for mortar. They said, Let's build a city for ourselves and a tower whose top will reach Heaven. They said, Let us make a name for ourselves. And the Lord came down from Heaven to see the tower which the people built. The Lord said, Behold, they are one people, and they have all the same language. This is what they have done and now nothing can stop them from performing unlimited advances. Now that I have explained this Biblical story to you, Karl, what is your immediate thought.''

"Sounds like a story."

"It is, Karl, and it was originally intended to be. It was written by Moses while he was in the desert with the Jews. The desert they were in was much more stark than eastern Oregon. They were camped in a particular spot for a great length of time. Moses decided to write stories for the children, and for the adults to teach the children how to read. Most people don't even know that Moses wrote the Book of Genesis.''

"I didn't. I thought he came about during Exodus.''

"A vast quantity of information has been lost over the years, especially why these books were written.''

"What was mostly lost, Eddie?''

"I can best explain by analyzing this story of Babel. First of all, common sense should tell you that if we all had one language, this language would be somewhat advanced. This being the case, why wouldn't God give equally advanced languages to all of mankind? Some language during Christ's time in Africa only had twenty to forty words. In your time, we could truly say that people living in jungles just didn't advance as fast, but the fact remains that they show no signs of ever having an advanced language. This leads to other facts. Why don't we have proof, archaeological finds, of a once-universal language? If Moses was trying to fool people, he wasn't smart enough. If he was trying to write so people could become literate, he did not have to say so at the time; they all knew these were stories. Moses was educated in Egypt. The Jews were slaves, let go, that had no education whatsoever. These were simple stories to simple people. These same people kept stories locked up. As

time passed, generation to generation, people blindly accepted these stories as truths. These people had no scientific methods or environment of
deductive reasoning. The stories were so filled with warning, the people
made a religion of them for reason of fear.''

"Like going to Hell, Eddie?''

"Exactly, Karl. These people thought much more crudely than even
you. Moses just wanted the kids to be good.''

"What a way to influence children; you're going to Hell if you
are bad.''

"We agree, Karl. The effect was good enough though; people were
much more well mannered and civil as a result of Moses' teachings.''

"Eddie, I do believe you concerning this particular story, but I do
believe a lot of what Moses wrote. What about the Book of Job? I always
heard a lot of this book.''

"Of all the books you had to ask me about, Karl, this one is the most
fictitious. This was a story to the slaves so they could learn discipline. You
have to understand that these same slaves were somewhat savage and
had little discipline once they were free. I will give you some insight
concerning the Book of Job. You recall the book starts out with Job being
described as a perfectly righteous person. I will quote to you a verse:
'Now there was a day when the angels of God came to present themselves
before the Lord. Satan also came among them, and the Lord said to Satan,
from where do you come? Then Satan replied and said, from roaming
about on Earth and walking around on it.'

"First of all, Karl, from the Bible we know that it says Satan waged
war on God prior to this and was thrown out of Heaven violently. Why
would he be allowed to mix in with the nonrebellious angels again, more
or less be permitted to re-enter Heaven? Second, why would God ask
him where he is coming from? This is obvious a story format written to
look as such. Then God continued friendly conversation with Satan,
asking him what he thinks of good old Job.''

"Yes, Eddie, I see your point. Sounds like a bedtime story.''

"If I was a human, Karl, I would not be able to sleep after hearing
this book, I would be frightened. Like I said, it was a story to help an
undisciplined people become upright and dignified. These people that
Moses himself was a racial member of, were disgusting to him. He had
to do something about his people, not only for reasons of their savagery,
but also he was embarrassed for them in the sight of Pharaoh. Moses had
something to prove, and he was a determined man. His desire to win

was fueled by his position of authority over the Jews; there were many thousands of them. They had never known a caring leader or a Jew with authority. Moses was a god in the eyes of all Jews.''

"This I understand, Eddie, and it makes sense. But from an evolutionist point of view, why does each country have a different language? Why are we different? Shouldn't have we all evolved the same?''

"Humans are physically different, Karl, but they are all of the same physical makeup when we speak of these original homelands. Black people coming from the African continent, Kenya for example, are a product of millions of years involving adaptation to their environment. The skin is black to prevent burning, an evolutionary trait at the molecular level. Not only is the skin black due to lack of shade and very direct sunlight, but their bodies are adapted to dissipate heat. These people are tall and have long extremities for cooling, like a radiator cools an engine. The long thin arms are cooled by the blood and easier heat dispersal. The blood brought back to the heart is cooler, keeping vital organs in the proper temperature zone. A man from Kenya has much more skin area that a man from the north, for example, an Eskimo. The Eskimo is short, stocky, and fatter to retain his body heat. This skin is lighter to help him get the vital sun rays, and as well does not need as much pigment for protection from the damaging rays. We know the sun does not shine so direct in Alaska, don't we, Karl?''

"Yes, this is interesting, I never thought of this before. So people like the Chinese are products of evolution based upon where they lived.''

"That is correct, Karl, the angle of sunlight in the millions of years past accounts for the slanted eyelids, which shielded the sun's rays off the retina. This area had more jungle and foliage for shade, which accounts for the slightly darker skin pigment. It also rained much, much more in the Far East than in Africa. The area was less harsh, temperature wise, so these people are generally shorter and smaller. The Chinese, or Oriental, is the medium between the Kenyan and Eskimo. The natural barriers that kept people separated generally had the effects of change on climate. For example, going from western Oregon's forest to eastern Oregon's sandy desert is a dramatic change. In such a short distance, even the deer are different on each side. Over further distances, languages were naturally different and at a different level, depending on the opportunity for greater intellectual advancement. Generally the medium climate was the better chance humans had at advancement, such as the Japanese or Europeans. Harsh climates kept people's ambitions down, to maintain a survival level that can be witnessed in these areas to this day."

"I really can understand this, Eddie, so these deer in eastern Oregon are different due to millions of years living and adapting to this specific environment."

"Yes, it started out at the molecular level of the deer. The proteins in the deer's ancestors were manufactured to produce a strand of DNA that would, over time, become totally adaptive to the environment."

"That's more than I can understand, Eddie. What I do understand is that it is just too hard for me to believe all this happened by chance."

"I understand, Karl; however, you are not aware of the actual statistics if you wish to speak of chance."

"What actual stats, Eddie?"

"There are literally trillions of stars in the universe, billions of them like the sun. The number is staggering, not to mention that just one in the many trillions produced a chance of life."

"I do agree, as I know trillions is very unimaginable in itself. Winning the lottery has much better odds than that."

"Ha, you are always at wit's end, Karl, no matter what the circumstances are."

"I have always been that way."

"I know, Karl."

"I'll laugh on my death bed, Eddie."

"No, you won't."

7

The Record Straight

The time is now 11000 B.C. on Earth, and we are moving forward through time in 1,000-year stages observing mankind's advances. The people of Earth are as diverse in race and the same in appearance as modern man. The only differences are body size and height. For the most part people are shorter and have light build, yet some are as tall and heavy as today. There are genetic disorders, birth defects, and many illnesses. The people are much more physically stronger, and are able to ward off the diseases that are so rampant. Most of the disease is bacterial and infects the digestive tract. Karl was struck by the fact that people would live their entire lives in a state of some sickness. He was aggravated to see these people sick from their being so naive. If only they could understand cleanliness, he thought. As more time passed by, he was surprised to see how fast the people were becoming aware of the correlation between filth and disease. This sense of filth and disease carried over to another way of life that angered him as much as he could ever recall.

They had become aware of possession and laid boundaries, which led them to believe in a sense of right and wrong. They associated that a clean body meant one was without wrong. If a person had a disease, he was treated as if sinful. They then invented gods, who would be worshiped by the killing and burning of animals. They said to these gods, We give our animal's life to you so you will give more life to us. They desired a more leisurely and material life. The civilizations that advanced faster by building cities and better shelters moved much farther ahead of the lesser, savage people. This was the result of their collective thinking combined with an improved man-made environment.

The advanced civilizations then needed more laborers to continue building cities. They took the closest savage people as slaves to do all hard labor. One of these civilizations was Egypt. Karl asked Eddie to show him Moses and the Hebrew slaves as it was.

"Karl, this is the purpose of our visit here, to set the record straight. You shall see every event from Moses to Christ's death. I have to ask you some questions first."

"What, Eddie?"

"At any point did you see a creator manufacture anything?"

"No, Eddie."

"Did you see a single man appear on Earth suddenly at a particular point in time?"

"No. I did see many people slowly appear from lesser and lesser animals."

"Did you see a man and woman in a garden where she gave the man an apple to eat which gave him knowledge?"

"Don't be funny, Eddie."

"I am not, Karl. I have to bring these things to your attention to make you think about what you are yet to see."

"I get it, and a lot more, too!"

"What do you get, Karl?"

"I get to realize how stupid I was to believe some story about a snake talking to a woman."

"About how an apple tree would open her eyes so she could see that she was naked, Karl?"

"I can't imagine myself ever buying into this!"

"Do not feel badly, Karl, many others have."

"But something so silly as a serpent and an apple tree got this far!"

"Leave it, Karl. Let it go. You were scared into believing something people made sacred and deemed it holy. If you showed outward rejection or disbelief, you would have been rejected, if not punished. I am going to show you Moses' life and his motives for writing the Testament. Some points you should be aware of are the order in which Moses wrote. He had many original writings he discarded, but he knew well of what his final writing would be. The Book of Exodus was started and near completion, he saw the troubles in the Hebrew camp and partially wrote the Book of Leviticus and the entire Book of Job. He then finished Exodus and through Deuteronomy. Genesis was the last book to be written. Moses was raised as a high-ranking Egyptian and was educated in all religious practices. All of his writings in the Bible concerning religious practice were in fact Egyptian practices. Come and see, Karl. We are 300 years before Moses' birth."

"I can understand why someone would write so extensively about this time, Eddie."

"You see the severity of mankind's oppression upon one another like never before or will ever be."

"The Egyptians killed the Hebrew men simply for enjoyment, and raped the women at will."

"What is the prime reason. Why, Karl?"

"The Egyptians have some knowledge, and the Hebrews are as close to simian behavior that is imaginable while being in human form. The Hebrew's speech is basically of survival only. They speak constantly of food, where to sleep, sex, and avoiding conflict with the Egyptians. When the Egyptians are present, the Hebrews bow down to them not only out of fear, but from total ignorance of who or what they are. They actually believe the Egyptians are a higher form of life. The Egyptians have to point the way for the Hebrews to understand, and beat them to make them remember a task. The only difference in training a dog is the physical beatings. The Hebrews were uneducated in simple domestic life. They did not bathe unless the Egyptians forced them in numbers into the rivers. Their sense of dignity was truly less than primordial; they would defecate openly and within feet of where they slept. When they became sick, they had no right to continue living, as they were deemed sinful and put to death by their own."

Eddie explained that Karl will see much more of this behavior while observing Moses' time.

"Karl, this will give you insight concerning the acceptance of the Bible during modern day. I have one last thing to show you involving the Egyptian behavior and their religious rituals. Look and see how they worship, Karl."

Karl saw priests and elders standing before an altar of fire. Behind the priests was a large stone table built on a large stone floor. There were seven steps up to this platform. Below was a very large walled area where any Egyptian is allowed to come in and worship. The elders brought in sheep, goats, and cattle. They first walked the cattle up onto the stone table. They stood on each side of the cow and stabbed it in the heart with long knives. The blood was collected in bowls and sprinkled over the fire. When they did this, all the worshippers went to their knees. They all began chanting at once, saying, The blood is the life of all flesh, and great are you almighty God.

They wiped up any excess blood that had fallen either on the table or floor with a white cloth and threw it into the fire while chanting again.

They then carefully removed the tissues and threw all the remains into the fire and chanted, "We return ourselves to you our loving God." They did the same with the sheep and goats. The goats were sacrificed to a separate god, a god they asked to leave them, and go to a far land and spread his affliction there. This god's name, translated into modern language, meant the destroyer, or devil. They had no name for the main god other than Almighty. There were other gods, and they made idols of them, but none of Almighty. Almighty was considered sacred and was to be found only in the people themselves. This God was too holy and great for a human to visualize so they did not attempt to carve a stone image of him.

Eddie said that Karl had seen all that was necessary.

"Come, Karl, look to Moses and the slaves. What do you see?"

The Hebrew slaves were in the very great number now and threatened Egypt in every circumstance, whether for food or an act of aggression. The pharaoh had ordered the newborns put to death, even though he feared the Hebrews. The labors had nearly stopped due to the cities being completed and refined over and over. The slaves were treated more humanly since there was little work for them, and more so since every Egyptian feared for his life. Hundreds of Egyptians had been killed by the Hebrews during stealthy night attacks on selected prepicked families.

Karl saw Moses speaking with Pharaoh about this problem. Moses was in fact a high priest in the top religious church, and Karl saw him giving the sacrifices. Moses' advice to Pharoh was to escort the Hebrews into the desert and abandon them. The pharaoh had regard for life, unlike the preceding rulers of Egypt, and this remark by Moses angered him. Pharaoh's words to Moses were, "I selected you from birth out of the Hebrew nation to have a seat amongst the gods with and for your own people! And now you wish to me to do this evil against them! No, Moses, you shall lead these people out of Egypt, and if you fail, I will make you a slave of slaves! Take your people to Canaan, conquer that land and defend it. You will act as my buffer against the kings of the East. You shall fight them first, not Egypt. Go take your people. I will follow you in the desert, killing the stragglers to make sure you leave entirely!"

Pharaoh ordered all the families and people of Egypt to give gifts to the Hebrews. Whatever the people had they gave generously to the Hebrews. They gave animals and food, gold and silver, and everything needed to make the journey across the desert. Pharaoh ordered this done so the Hebrews would go in peace as he feared this move could turn on him.

Pharaoh took Moses to the place where all the Hebrews knew Moses and his position as religious mediator between Jew and Egyptian. The people accepted Moses. Then Pharaoh blessed all the Jews, but his blessing and wishes of their wealth were spurious. The Hebrews were enraptured to leave Egypt and had Moses lead them with his brother Aaron following behind.

After Moses led the people for one half-day's journey into the desert, he founded a plan that would ensure the Jews loyalty to him. Moses spoke to the people, telling them a lie, saying, "We must flee quickly, for it is Pharaoh's plan to trap us in the wilderness and kill all men and children. He shall take our women back to Egypt and sacrifice them to the gods."

The Hebrews took him at his word and hurried their journey and daily lives, including making unleavened bread, their staple food, to save more time.

After a few days, the Egyptians sent out a battalion of soldiers on chariots, and they caught up to the Hebrews. From there they killed scores of Jews, but the Jews came back in number upon seeing few chariots. They killed all the drivers and soldiers, took the horses, and threw the chariots into what they called the Red Sea or Sea of Reeds, but is now known as part of the modern day Suez Canal.

After this, no Jew would question Moses as a true leader, even though it was in his heart to abandon them in the desert. He could no longer hold to this solution of eliminating them, as he had no place to go and live peacefully. Moses soon realized his power, and this he decided to use selfishly, for himself. Moses found that the Jews believed he spoke to God, and God to him. He used this to gain complete control over the Hebrew people. He was constantly saying, "Thus says the Lord your God," preceding everyday orders he wished to give. The people obeyed without hesitation. But the people were extremely undisciplined and needed constant teaching.

Moses wrote down hundreds of laws while in the desert. Many of them so simple, Karl was finally convinced that the Bible was not the all-time universal code book of life. For example, Moses walked through the camp and saw how people would defecate openly in the camp near places they would slaughter animals and eat. From this he made a law of God, saying that people are to leave the camp when they have to relieve themselves, and take a shovel with them to cover the feces. This law remained in his writings and found its way into the Bible in Deuteronomy 23:12–13. He stated also that the Hebrews were the chosen ones, deemed holy by God and that God walked through the camp. God would punish them for this since Jehova was pure and could not see this ugliness to remain pure.

Moses himself was not truly aware of the Hebrew culture. He had visited the Hebrew camps during the slavery years in Egypt but did not become involved with them. Now that he lived with them, they were completely a disgusting people in his or anyone's eyes. He decided to lead them to a place in the desert that he could isolate himself. This area was called Mount Horeb. Here Moses commanded them to wait for him while he spoke to God. Moses would go up into the mountains for over a month and write rules, laws, and rituals to be performed. Moses had to make very tedious and cumbersome rules for the Jews to live by. One of these rules is found in the Bible, Book Leviticus 81:23, "You shall not have sex with any animal to be defiled with it, nor shall any women stand before an animal to mate with it, it is a perversion." This rule was given to the Jews, since they were having intercourse with cattle, goats, sheep, and other animals. The rules were not given by God. They were given simply by Moses to a savage people. The rules are explicit and detailed of already occurring behavior. For example, the men would order the women to stand in front of dogs or other animals, nude and fondle the animals sexually to the point of a dog having external or internal ejaculations. The hideousness of this did not rattle Moses nearly as much as today's people would be repulsed. He was somewhat crude as well, and partially related to some of the Hebrew culture. He believed in hard alcohol and drank excessively. This was partially exposed in Deuteronomy 14:26. He also referred to Noah, who never existed, as being very drunk, with the implication that this was not a sin.

"Eddie, you said that Noah never existed, what about these so-called discoveries of the ark?"

"There has truly been no ark discovery. What you have seen on television is religious sects promoting this with lavish detail to gain members. The purpose of this propaganda is to collect tithes from new believers. Something as big as a confirmed ark discovery would certainly create a new wave of Christian and Zionist faith movements never before seen. However, the church has been unable to convince the people as a whole

102

due to the lack of hard evidence needed to convince the people. Believe me, Karl, a great deal of truth comes out of the small tabloids, but something as enormous as discovering the ark would be on the huge networks. You would see this all over the national news, Peter Jennings would be discussing this on world news, not some bystander preacher.''

''I knew that! Why didn't I think of that before?''

''For the same reason all do, no one is willing to challenge something deemed so holy and sacred.''

''This is why the Bible and other religious beliefs hang with us, isn't it? We are afraid of these things, aren't we?''

''Yes, very afraid, but you don't need to challenge all this with fear if you use the facts.''

''What facts?''

''Take, for example, the actual circumstances concerning the writing of Noah in the Book of Genesis. We can safely say this all occurred about 4500 years ago or so, more or less, from a theoretical point. The actual time according to Moses' text is about the 3500 year range, but we will stay with 4500 to be safe. If world population is a little over five billion in the 1990s, how long would it take to get to that number from one family?''

''I don't know Eddie.''

''A great deal longer, Karl. The world population could not even come close to this figure. Also there are obvious facts that utterly destroy Moses' story. One is all the different races on the earth and the population concentrations of these races.''

''I don't understand, Eddie?''

''The Chinese alone are a different race than the supposed Noah family. How could this race come about so abruptly and with such extreme facial differences. The Chinese are in mass numbers compared to the rest of the world. It is a mathematical impossibility for the Chinese to have been Noah's descendants, along with the Africans and absolutely anyone else in such a short time.''

''Oh, man. Eddie, you really blew the lid on this. Why haven't I ever been told these things?''

''Why would anyone wish to talk about such things? First, to humans this is boring, and second, the church would never promote anything close to this.''

''This makes me think about the animals on the ark. You know, there are a lot of different animals in different places around the world, like kangaroos in Australia, a country surrounded by water. Why is the kangaroo there and not in the places closer to where the ark landed?''

"Because they evolved in Australia, Karl. You know that."

"Moses also said something I know is not true. He said that it didn't rain before this. That is a scientific impossibility."

"Are you sure, Karl?"

"Absolutely. The fossil records around the world proves this, along with many other proofs such as the Grand Canyon alone."

"I think you are suddenly more on the reality side of life, Karl."

"All it takes is proof, some kind of evidence. I can't believe I didn't think about all the other races and obvious evidence to clarify this."

"You couldn't think that way, Karl. The rest of your society had you trapped on a grand scale of conformity to their ways, which in fact is perilous to question. But that is all beginning to change now. Science is in fact beginning to rule in the minds of people worldwide. This science is education and is your only hope of survival."

"So Noah never really existed?"

"Neither did Job. Come on, Karl, do you really think if Noah did exist that he was the only good person on the planet, or even that this god of yours would just say screw it and kill everyone instead of using reason with his creation?

"There are hundreds of serious, openly known, fallacies to the stories of Moses, but people who chose to believe him are convinced due to the difficulty in reading the Bible. In the case of the Flood and Noah, there were only nine generations from Adam and Eve to Noah's birth. The believers cannot correlate that there could be only a handful of people on the earth at the time of the Flood. On top of this, they cannot connect God's out-of-the-way decision to destroy so few people with such a unprecedented and grand scale operation of flooding the planet. According to Moses' story, there could have been no more than a few hundred people living. I won't get into where Cain's wife came from and other extreme holes in Moses' stories, as the believers state that the Book is not meant to be taken literally. If it isn't meant to be taken literally, then why was it written? Why do we find precise statements such as in Genesis 9:18–19, 'The three sons of Noah—Shem, Ham, and Japeth—from these the whole earth was populated.' We know from carefully studied human population growth rates, it would have taken millions of years to reach our current count of over five billion."

104

"I have heard it said that the Flood was not worldwide but confined to the area in question."

"Oh, Karl, don't fall into this trap of maladjusting as you go to strengthen your hopes and unwarranted dreams! Come on, what does the story of Moses actually say about the scale of the Flood?"

"Says that the whole earth was flooded, and not one living thing on the land lived, and like you said, Noah's sons were responsible for populating the entire earth."

"Not to mention, Karl, the story says that the ark came to rest on Mount Ararat. If that were true, the immediate area of Noah's home would have been covered in an impossible amount of water. There simply is not enough water on Earth to cover it to this depth. If the polar ice caps melted and all sources of water were released, the level wouldn't come close to twenty percent of this story's miscalculation. But I will not argue these points. As I said, the believers will say God made this possible. I will argue the facts, such as of Moses' sons and the other races. The Chinese have been around a lot longer than Moses or Noah."

"You're angry, Eddie."

"Of course I am. Do you know how many of your kind have used these stories to say God told me to kill my wife, or go crazy in Waco. I will quote a small passage Moses used to keep women from men's shortcomings. Deuteronomy 25:11–12, If a woman stretches out her hand and seizes a man's genitals while he is in a fight with her husband, then you shall cut off her hand. You shall not show pity. Forget that Moses is controlling women; we've already discussed that. The problem is in modern day society. When some people read this, they interpret God in a way that allows them to do insane actions, such as blowing up buildings filled with babies or soldiers and deny that it was terrorism but rather divine direction. Another example of this terrible way of leading people is found in Deuteronomy 22:24, You shall purge the evil from among you. Interestingly, the preceding text mentions that you shall put to death a woman rape victim because she did not cry out. Sound like a modern-day rape trial scenario, Karl?"

"I have known about these things. I mean, people who seriously screw up because they get engrossed in God."

"It isn't that simple, Karl. Children reading this stuff don't forget it. This is hard impact material that does change thinking processess because they have no choice but to accept the Bible. Many otherwise good people would not have caused harm to others if it weren't for these

Bible teachings. I and others don't give a damn about Noah and the ark. What we hate is the direct and deceitful misuse of authority. Moses took the job on of leading the people. If he couldn't do it honestly and with correct human diplomacy, he should have stepped down. I will grant that during this time, it was most difficult to manage people, especially those out in the desert, but this is no reason to wrack the mental condition of an already suffering population. Imagine that you are a rape victim worried about the stoning death you may be facing if you didn't scream out loud enough.''

It was becoming clear to Karl what factual point Eddie was trying to show him. That God did not make these laws. Rather a desperate man had to save face for his people. The entire countryside was watching Moses—many people, including the Egyptians.

Nevertheless, Karl wished to observe Moses the most, to find out what kind of man he was. Eddie pointed out specific laws and writings to him, exposing Moses.

"Karl, I shall read to you from the Holy Bible concerning some words that show how Moses thought.

"From Deuteronomy 25:7–9: 'If a man does not desire to take his dead brother's wife, then his brother's wife shall go up to the gate of the elders and say, ''My husband's brother refuses to establish a name for his brother in Israel. He is not willing to marry me.'' The elders of his city shall summon him and speak to him. If he persists and says no, I do not desire her, then the brother's wife shall come to him in sight of the elders, and pull off *his shoe* from his right foot, *and spit* in his face. His name shall be called the house of him whose shoe is removed.' To iterate on the lighter of this law of Moses, I will relate to your time, Karl, a phrase that is coined as one who 'wears the pants in the house.'

"In these early days, the one who wore shoes was the working authority. To have someone remove his shoes then would be the same as having your pants removed publicly. Shoes were more important to them, as you can see, they needed them to work more than they did pants. Indecency was not an issue here or in your time; rather, it is humiliation. The severity of spitting in a man's face was Moses' solution for the woman to feel vindicated for her own feelings of rejection. There was considerable circumstances of husbands dying. Widows became a problem for Moses.

"There was no compassion in Moses for the women. He just made up rules that were *easy* as he went. It was easy for Moses to make a rule; he only needed a solution. There was no genuine care for the women, the children, or for the sake of Israel. Moses' law stemmed from two areas of his life. One of them being the great responsibility he had for these people. Since this workload was so great, he manufactured statements to ease his work and stress. Moses did whatever worked. Second, Moses was truly a callous person from his childhood. He was brought up in a pompous, businesslike environment, and he never had a chance to experience love. His life was never simple enough to sit down and play, more or less hold someone in his arms. At no time did Moses ever walk with a girl, holding hands, while in Egypt.

Because of his lack of love, he was able to reel off ruthless and frightening commands. Moses could not understand the brother's lack of love for his dead brother's wife from his own lack of love in depth and in general. Moses could only relate to a man being with a woman and raising a family. His understanding of love for one another was quite superficial. One shall ask themselves whether this rule was in fact a commandment of God, if so, why does it not *cling to our way* of thinking or living. The rational and reasonable mind informs that if you don't love someone, the relationship will contain multiple flaws. It is safe to say that you don't have to be forced to love your dead brother's wife, and sacrifice your life.

"Moses also incorporated rules into his writings in a dramatic way and to appear as a result of the people's sins and wrongfulness. In Genesis 3:16, Moses says that God spoke directly to Eve, admonishing her for disobedience. God says 'because you have sinned, I will greatly multiply your pain in childbirth. In pain you shall bring forth children, yet your desire shall be for your husband, and he shall rule over you.' The women blamed the men and held them responsible for the labor pain in childbirth. They were coming up with ideas to make men suffer by any means. The women were also feeling independent as a result of being freed slaves. Moses didn't savvy either of these liberal thorns, so he cleverly came up with Genesis 3:16. Women were to blame, and they owed homage to men for their sins. What a wonderful solution to push a poor unknowledgeable people around in the desert. Moses did not only use his cleverness for power but also for recognition from other nations. The Book of Genesis was written to give Moses a background or lineage. He wrote this book to give the Jews a name with dignity as he realized they would be viewed as having nothing and be seen as savage pigs.

"He fabricated Genesis not only to look like the Hebrew were people with a background, but that they were the first lineage directly created and chosen by God! The ramification of this fabrication flaunts at the height of betrayal to all other races of mankind. It is no wonder that people all over the earth not only hate Jews but have literally tried the genocide of these people. This driving force over the centuries has been constant and has been mistaken for an evil force. This force is simply the oneness of mankind venting an imperfect punishment on a sore in the body of humanity. Even in the goodness of mankind's oneness, there is still imperfection and hatred, which has caused this invited admonishment of Jewish people.''

Eddie let Karl move about to observe Moses. As time passed, some of the Jews began questioning Moses about God. He was getting old, and none of the people had seen this God he spoke of. No one questions Moses' leadership, only his relations with God. Moses later appointed priests from the camp that were loyal to him. By giving some authority to a few more people, Moses created a temporary boundary between him and the skeptics. Time eventually ran out for Moses, and the people sided with Aaron in a month-long rebellious party. They returned to the savage ways and many engaged in excess heterosexual and homosexual activity, including sodomy of all kinds. They melted down the gold and made idols and chanted to a god they knew in Egypt. The name of this god, translated, meant free will, a strong desire they always had and pursued for hundreds of years. They continued sacrificing and followed Moses as a leader.

''Moses left the camp and climbed Mount Horeb. Moses knew he would regain the people's confidence as Aaron was no match as a leader, and also, Moses had some tricks up his sleeve.

''Moses carved out laws on stone tablets he had made. He painted his face white, which was an Egyptian ritual to frighten evil spirits. Moses climbed back down Horeb into sight of the Hebrews. When they saw him, he acted out his ability as an authority with all that he was. He screamed at them that God is giving them their last chance; these tablets were his mercies now they are broken for you to sift through. Moses then threw the tablets off a high rock and they shattered. He told Aaron to come up and speak with him. Aaron feared for his life, seeing Moses' white face and thinking God did in fact speak to him. Moses yelled at Aaron, telling him to crawl on his hands and knees and not to look at him. Aaron came within about fifty feet of Moses, bowing down before him. Moses commanded him to melt down the idols and grind them into powder and mix it with water and make the people drink it. Moses went all the way on this one, striking at the center of these people's fear. Moses instructed Aaron that he would go back to Mount Horeb and plead with God not to abandon the Hebrew nation. He said that when he returned, the people shall cleanse themselves and follow all the laws or he would call fire out of heaven to destroy them. Moses' warnings were strengthened by a severe electrical storm, which the people mistook for God's anger.

At this point, Karl no longer believed in an unseen God. He could not see God anywhere on this planet. All he saw was the ignorance of mankind in its infancy. He thought if aliens visited this planet at this time, they would actually kill all these people as if they were animals of sport. All that he saw from the beginning of the universe, to Earth's ending, combined with human behavior during this supposed Bible era confirmed to him that God was a fable. It would have not been necessary for Eddie to show him creation and the future. All he had to see was these people to make him disbelieve in God. Even if he did not see Moses lying to the people, he wouldn't have decided any different.

At this point, he told Eddie that he didn't want to see any more of these people. Karl turned away with a strong detestation of early man.

"Karl, you despair over these people to the point of exhaustion."

"Eddie, just coming from the twentieth century is enough, but you have shown me paradise of the future. To experience this savagery and perversion of the past is devastating to human feelings of integrity."

"I am not disappointed in you, Karl. After I show you something of yourself and all of mankind, you will wish to see the past more so than you originally desired."

"What do you wish to show me, Eddie?"

"What I wish to show you, you must also personally experience, Karl. This will take time, and you will suffer extensively. However, I shall bring you back and restore you."

"Bring me back from where!"

"You have to be fully aware in the mind of what it is that made man look to or seek a god."

"I am not feeling too keen about this, Eddie. What exactly are you asking me to do?"

"You are to become one of the past humans by being born into a primitive family."

"I will not subject myself to this evil savagery or be one of these slaves."

"I am not asking that of you, Karl, but that you would be born into a tribe of humans in the year 50,000 B.C."

"You want me to become a caveman?"

"Yes."

"Why?"

"When you return from living this primitive life, you shall remember completely your entire experience, your emotions, and your entire being. This life shall not become a part of your current life in the sense of being degraded. You will still retain your character, but have the knowledge of primitive life and thinking."

"You're saying I am going to be reborn and live a new life, from scratch, without any knowledge of ever living before?"

"Yes, Karl."

"This will show me why people started believing in gods?"

"Completely and deeply within yourself."

"This does intrigue me, Eddie. As I think about it, it sounds more like opportunity than suffering."

"Like I said before, Karl, you are an optimist."

"How long will I live in this time, Eddie?"

"About thirty-six years, Karl."

"Will it seem long?"

"When you will have returned, Karl, the time will seem to have been lost, but not much. It will be enough for you to realize the full effect of your journey. The thirty-six years that you will actually live will seem as a very long time. Time shall drag to you, and pain and hunger will be a part of everyday living. Do you want to go and live this life?"

"I know you will bring me back, Eddie."

"Till we meet again, Karl."

As with any memory of one's life, Karl cannot remember his infancy before he was two and a half years old. The senses of sight, smell, and hearing became much more keen. All he could absorb were what he saw, smelled, or felt. He saw the person who was his mother as one who took care of him. He could not and never would be able to relate words or thoughts to her. He only recognized her by her image and her scent. He could recognize all people he came into contact with this same way.

When he was older, he related to these people by their scents. After he recognized them, he would recall their disposition. If he smelled a hostile male, he would hide before he could find him or his caretaker.

He did not know she gave birth to him. He did not understand life or death. He only knew that this person cared for him, and the place he lived went from brightness to darkness. He could not understand the day and night; at the age of five, he only knew it happened and what to expect in the darkness and the light. When he was seven, he experienced the emotion of love for his mother when she held him.

At age eight, he met another boy who lived in the ground under a large tree. His caretaker was friendly, like Karl's mother. She followed him to his mother, who was gathering food. They all were initially cautious of each other but curious. They became closely knit friends after running into each other several more times. They had plenty of food from the trees and bushes, so there was no contention. His friend and his mother showed him how to dig in the ground under a big rooted tree for the same kind of shelter they had. His mother and he had no permanent home; they roamed about. This shelter was small pelts from animals that his mother had killed. She was a good hunter. She would usually tree the animals and climb up and spear them.

They would wrap themselves up together in the furs at nightfall or when cold weather came. They knew that wrapping themselves up would camouflage their scent as well. They were aware that animals did not come to the smell of dead fur or pelts. The animals that sought after dead flesh were afraid of humans and fled. They were constantly on guard for larger flesh-eating animals. He only knew this from seeing his mother's caretaker, or husband, killed by a lion. He was seven years old when that happened. Like his mother, he did not understand him to be her husband or the concept of him being his father. It was purely visual and scent recognition when this man came around occasionally and sometimes brought food. He was independent and did not at any time live with them. He would not do anything that a modern father would do, such as tickle him or play. He was aware of his being his mother's child but did not relate him as a result of his intercourse with her. He had a natural fear of him and avoided his mother when he was there.

As he grew he became more independent and left his mother. He saw her frequently for two years, then he began to venture farther away from his forest homeland. His friend and he hunted together all their lives. They learned how to track animals and techniques to corner large prey between them for the kill.

He would visualize his mother and where they lived. He missed her deeply at times, but for the most part, he was busy surviving. He had an inner sense of security knowing she was there. He had no real concept of her dying, especially of old age; even after seeing death, he did not understand, because he had no relations with people before they died and did not need them or expect anything from them. He expected his mother to be there for him. As time passed, he wanted to do for her what she did for him. He searched her out with his friend.

They spent several weeks looking in the forest for both their mothers. His friend knew this was what he wanted to do when he returned to the forest and found their empty shelters. They split up and looked to all the places were their mothers hunted. They knew to meet back at the shelter when darkness came. Their scent of one another was strong and well identified due to their lengthy partnership, so it would be difficult to lose each other permanently. If he was down wind from him several miles, his scent was detectable. They used this technique when looking for their mothers. Several days passed without locating them, so they hunted the area for food and lived their lives day-by-day in the forest.

One day he was hunting on his own, as he frequently did, when his friend came to him frantically waving his arms. He caught his scent and another scent he was carrying, but it was vague to him. His friend came close and rubbed his hands on Karl's face. He recognized his mother's scent immediately and grabbed him with both hands, joyous, and insisted on looking in the forest to find his mother. He pointed with his arm extended. Karl ran along with him until exhausted, then pushed himself half-a-day's walk. When he found her, he experienced many emotions. The love for her was deep, yet he was shocked to see her looking different, he did not understand the aging process at all, since he, like others, were so independent of other humans. She was so ecstatically happy to see him that he felt completely secure within himself.

She was living with a group of women; some were his age. They prepared food and made large fires to dance about. That evening, his mother took him into a dugout where there was a girl about the age of twenty. His mother had brought some of the fire into the dugout to provide light for them. She hugged the girl and pointed to him and touched her sexually. The girl looked at him with both desire and a trace of fear. He felt the same way as she, but certainly did not know what to do sexually. His mother put them together, face to face, while standing. She put their arms around each other, and they both found enjoyment and held each other tightly. She pressed them down to the floor and physically kept them holding each other, then left. He felt an insecurity when his mother left, but the girl held him. They continued all evening to hold each other face-to-face and touching their nude bodies together and exploring the exhilarating feeling of sex. He discovered intercourse with her that evening. She was a virgin but had more knowledge of what his body parts were for than he did. They became the new residents of the dugout, but his friend and he made new dugouts and filled them with twice the furs for their very appreciative mothers. They built the new dugouts away from the ones they lived in, as the other women desired to live away from men, and by themselves.

Sharing life with the girl was easy. They both hunted, sometimes together, and equally apart. For the most part, hunting depended on who was the most hungry, but they shared their food because of their love for one another and spent all their free time loving each other. They had food, shelter, love, and sex, making them blissfully happy.

The relationship with his male friend became stark; however, they remained friendly when they ran into each other while hunting. His friend died from infection to a wound about four months after he found his mother and had taken a woman as his companion. His woman companion stayed where they both had lived. She mourned for him, crying constantly and hunted only when her hunger became overwhelming. She was four months' pregnant, as was Karl's woman. Some of the other women brought her food when her unhappiness brought her close to starvation. She left the area a month later and was never seen again. Some of the women, including the mother, looked in her dugout daily and cried for her occasionally.

Karl's companion was now eight months' pregnant and continued to hunt and work. The people, including him, understood what was occurring when a woman was with child. They just did not correlate sexual intercourse with pregnancy. Giving birth was a womanly calling, separate from a man. After a birth, the woman cared for the child, and the man was generally pushed away by the other women who cared for the mother.

The women all cared for his companion during her ninth month, as she did no hunting during this month. He did the hunting for her; however the women's bond was too strong for him to gain entry with his small contributions. He built a shelter in the trees from animal furs to watch over the situation. He missed being with his woman in every way. He knew that it would be different now, as he had seen how the mothers had taken care of their children after birth. He now realized who his mother was. He felt compelled to leave but remained to see the child.

Karl's whole world of expectation for his woman and the unborn child were shattered when both she and the child died during labor. He was too broken in spirit to live any longer himself after the happiness this woman gave him. He wandered from the camp and hunted the grounds where his male friend and he had hunted for several years before coming back to his mother.

Karl returned five years later to this camp and found his mother. His mother was old and weak; her hunting skills had diminished radically. No one would help her, only he. He brought her food every day and looked after her during most of his free time.

She died during the winter of that year. She was too weak to maintain her body temperature. This time was the worst for him. No one was there for him, and he knew no one; he had been a loner.

He stayed in the camp and lived his life hunting and making the dugout a better place to live. He smoothed the walls with stone and completely lined his shelter with furs. When it rained, the water would run off, as he discovered how to divert it outside by a drainage trench. He taught the other women this and gained favor with them. Before this, they had a low level of animosity toward him. They had shunned him wherever he was, even if he came around them. He felt a semi-state of peace; at least he was around and in a camp of people.

The women generally built a very large fire each evening. They would place meat from any kind of animal they caught and butchered close to the fire. After the meat was cooked, they ate and threw the excess into the fire. He saw them bow down toward the fire every evening, but he did not know what this meant. One evening he stayed in his dugout and several of the women came in. They took him by the hand and led him to the fire and gave him what looked like venison meat. They placed their shares of meat before the fire, and so he did to be in conformity. He watched them closely and did as they did. After several weeks of doing this, he felt bonded with these women as a genuine partaker in this ritual. He did not wish to lead in this nightly ceremony, as some of the women did; he feared these people and knew they would harm him if he showed any position other than doing as told.

Shortly after this, some of the women, who were probably twenty-eight to thirty years old, came into his dugout after the ceremonies. These women came in pairs. While one watched the entrance, the other would seduce him into intercourse. In the beginning he was frightened, within two weeks he waited for them to come rather than try to sleep first. The women were fascinated with his male sex organs and his masculine body. They became so intrigued with him, that they bowed on their knees to him. He no longer hunted or did any work, as the women looked after his needs. This was very difficult for him to understand in the beginning. He tried to hunt for his own food, but they would not let him. His food was always placed in his shelter morning and evening. They continued to have sex with him, more and more frequently. His body was very strong, and he had a voracious sexual appetite after these women had started this behavior. There were many women who still shunned him, and he gained a sense of fear of these women, feeling that they would overthrow him in the camp.

There is still no language or thinking process concerning words. Life is lived by the senses, understanding people's behavior toward you is judged by sight. The judgment was usually from facial expressions of anger or interest toward you. The women who shunned him showed little interest, but what little there was reflected a mild unsettling.

Two months later, a group of thirty to forty strong men came through the camp early in the morning. He caught their scent long enough in advance to climb a tall tree where he had recently made a lookout. He had enjoyed sitting in the tree looking over the land. This day he would not enjoy his view, as these men battered the women and raped them. Some took women with them when they left that afternoon. One of the men had been seriously injured in the initial attack by several women and was left behind. There were more women, but these men carried rocks and heavy clubs, which kept the women at bay. Several women were killed that morning.

The women picked themselves up and reunited shortly after the attack, seemingly as though this had happened before. They built a much larger fire than before and placed the man close to the fire as they had done with the meat. They each ate some of his flesh and the other meat as well. They then dismembered him and threw his carcass into the fire.

The women who did not accept Karl became loud and showed signs of attacking his shelter. He had been too frightened to come down from the lookout all day. Some of his loyal women held off the rebellious women, but only momentarily. At a sudden moment the entire camp ran to his dugout ripping the furs out and destroying the shelter violently. They set fire to the dugout and searched frantically for him. It was not long before they figured out where he was, knowing his lookout was there. He climbed down seconds before they got there, since he knew

115

they would come there next. They did see him and gave pursuit. He knew the route to his hunting grounds well and lost them in the darkness. He understood why they wanted to do harm to him, and also why many men and women lived independently.

There was no comfort for him anywhere now other than the weather being warm and food plentiful. He gathered fruits, berries, and other plant food during the spring and summer months. He tried to enter a few male camps, only to be pushed out. The population consisted of at least ninety percent loners, and the rest were loose-knit camps as the one he came from; this was in the sense that each person did his own hunting and work. He still needed this loose companionship as he had always had someone around him. Now, being alone made him emotionally miserable, which intensified when people either harmed or rejected him.

The days and weeks dragged on with memories of the friends he had haunting him constantly. He felt lonely in all his daily calamity of hunting and seeking shelter. He had become injured in the late fall while making chase in a hunt. His left shoulder was severely dislocated and he fractured the elbow joint. He handled the pain quite well but was unable to move quickly enough to catch his prey. The winter was coming, and the plant food was rapidly diminishing. He fed himself just about anything edible to fight the hunger. All during this time he looked to the sky at day and stars by night. He wondered who could help him. He knew he was very close to what had happened to his mother, death.

Each day he felt more lonely and began wanting to believe in something. He began to fervently reach out to a god, something, someone. He could not accept being alone. In an intense moment before he knew of his death, he verbally let out a humble mercy cry from his heart to the stars, hoping someone would come save him. He fell into a dark sleep after feeling his face rest in the mud. He had a dream: he was walking down Franklin Boulevard in Eugene. He saw Dunkin Donuts where Sandi had worked. When he walked by, he saw her inside. She looked up at that moment, and with a kind, interested eye, she stood up. He continued to walk straight, following her eye contact for a second. Without looking, he knew she came running out the front door. He was past the shop, and she ran out to the sidewalk behind him.

She softly called out. This made him feel a great peace, then he awoke. Someone was holding him.

"Hello, Karl."

"Hi, Eddie."

8

Human Reality

"Do you know where I was?"

"I was there the whole time."

"I was an animal, Eddie!"

"You were, Karl. Not now."

"Was it predestined? Did you know exactly what I was going to go through?"

"No, not in the sense of being predestined. I did allow for you to be injured though."

"You knew I would search for God from this suffering."

"People still do that, Karl."

"Yes, but this was at the most primitive level. I couldn't even think. I barely associated."

"Did you really believe in God then, when you were alone, Karl?"

"I had no choice, Eddie, yes, I wanted to believe so badly in God that I made something from nothing. Is that what happened to other people, people in Moses' time, people of our time?"

"I believe so."

"You have first-hand experience, Karl, not only from your cry to God, but didn't you see the women worshipping the fire?"

"Yes, Eddie, you are right. They invented God. I invented God."

"Does that seem entirely different from the future people creating SB: 1, or God?"

"I created God in mind; they created God with their knowledge and hands."

"Did you feel comforted after you created God in your mind, Karl?"

"Yes, I was partially satisfied in my belief."

"How much more satisfied do you think you would be if you created a superbeing with all of mankind's help. The superbeing retained what you are and was able to become perfect."

"I would never worry about life again."

"Karl, do not be concerned about what people believe in. I will remind you that you do not have to believe anything concerning a God, just believe in humanity. If you wish to believe in Christ, or anyone else, do so earnestly. It is not a concern that people of your time believe in SB: 1."

"What is the purpose of all this then?"

"To prepare the people for that time in their lives when they meet SB: 1 and realize who SB: 1 really is."

"You mean when they meet who they think is God."

"They will be prepared for his coming, Karl. The people will have prime knowledge. Whether they believe it or not, this awareness will help them accept some dramatic truths, such as the stories of Moses."

"Then the whole purpose of a prerevelation is to avoid shocking people."

"There are so many weak people in the twentieth century, Karl. SB: 1 and the council have derived a plan to ease the world into resurrection with minimal hardship. It was decided to reveal this information from within twentieth century people. You are among the first to take this information and publicize it worldwide. Few will accept anything you speak of, and your life shall be threatened. Many revealing events shall take place over time, bringing the people closer to this truth. Then other people shall come forward, many being phony, but the true teachers will show evidence. If any of these speakers asks for money contributions, they are false. Giving is true humanity; taking is treason."

"I am coming closer to the truth, Eddie. I am understanding humanity as a whole. You used the word 'treason', I understand that you mean treason against the family of humans. We truly must accept and love each other."

"Your words can be said much simpler, Karl."

"In which way, Eddie."

"Be at peace with one another. Do you know who first said this, Karl?"

"No."

"Jesus Christ."

"What about Jesus, Eddie?"

"Do you really wish to know him, Karl?"

"I thought I did once. I was a Christian as a young man. You have proved differently though, Eddie."

118

"No, I have not, Karl."

"What do you mean?"

"Let me show you someone who lives in your time."

"I would love to see anybody of my time."

"Do you remember Veronica?"

"Veronica? You mean from church when I was in Germany?"

"Yes, Karl, you knew her for nearly three years."

"She was a good Christian."

"Would you like to see her?"

"Yes! I loved her! She was great."

"You loved her as a Christian friend."

"We were the best friends ever. We never did anything wrong. We didn't even kiss."

Eddie took Karl to a church he attended and worked at in Germany while he was in the army.

"Do you remember this old church on Fliegerhorst Kaserne, Karl?"

"How could I forget. I spent every Sunday here."

"You and Veronica would go to this coffee house on Friday nights."

"We would make the evening hors d'oeuvres and show a movie to all the brothers and sisters who were for real."

"What made you decide these Christians were more real than the mediocre group who just attended Sunday worship, Karl?"

"We were the charismatic, Eddie. We have the spirit. We would speak in unknown tongues and be baptized in the Holy Spirit. We were all so close to each other and really had a love for life in God."

"So you believe God was inside you more as a result of these things."

"Eddie, we were dedicated. We had Jesus in our hearts. We had peace."

"Where did you have your peace, Karl?"

"In our hearts, especially when we were together."

"What was it like when you were working around the non-Christian?"

"It was hell. They really ranked on me hard. Some came very close to assaulting me. The military leaders held me back, and my closest peers that I roomed with totally avoided me."

"Is this real peace, Karl?"

"You have made me realize something for the first time. Maybe it was just me, my personality."

"How do people in general treat you now, or more, how did they treat you before you converted to Christianity?"

"The same people in Germany liked me very much, we did all kinds of things together. I get along very well with people today."

"What if you mention Jesus to someone now?"

"You mean stick up for Jesus because I believe in him."

"Yes."

"They are negative about it most of the time."

"How many people came into your church and found this peace, then went back to their own ways?"

"I guess most all of them, Eddie, none lasted, now that I think about it."

"Wasn't that some indication to you that God was not all that powerfully bonding in true love, Karl?"

"I did think that, yes. I thought if God was true to people and he showed it to them, they could not walk away so easily."

"Then this program failed constantly."

"It did with them, Eddie."

"Why didn't it fail with you so fast, Karl?"

"Because I truly believed in Christ."

"So, was it Christ, Karl?"

"I don't know, I did feel so good in those days though, real good. It was love and peace."

"Let us look at Veronica, Karl."

"She is worshipping God, Eddie. She has her hands lifted over her head thanking and praising Jesus. Look at the peace in her eyes and her smile. She is truly happy, Eddie."

"I don't disagree with you, Karl, but may I please show you the past twelve hours of her life."

"Why?"

"I need to prove where her happiness is coming from, Karl."

"Show me, then."

Eddie took him to Veronica's house that evening.

"Tell me what you see, Karl."

"I see Veronica in her living room with a man I'd met once with her before. I can tell that they live together. I never knew she had a male friend, Eddie."

"He is her live-in boyfriend, Karl. They have been together for two years."

"That means she met him after she was in the church."

"Why would you be concerned about that, Karl?"

"I know that some people who were tied up with a lover before converting would have some serious problems breaking off the relationship."

"Especially a woman convert, Karl."

"I can't say for a fact, Eddie, but I've seen it all too often, not just for Christian sake either."

"So this live-in boyfriend is viewed as something she delved into against policy then."

"Yes, it is, even from her point, since I heard her speak this very same policy herself, Eddie."

"Continue watching her, Karl."

They were smoking cigarettes, drinking alcohol to excess and then smoked marijuana. She used foul language constantly and talked of sex. She was not crude, but rather comical about their behavior. They began to have sex. Eddie and Karl pulled out of Veronica's life.

"I'm surprised, Eddie. I never would have suspected or thought Veronica was a hypocrite."

"She is not, Karl."

"Eddie, I saw her, as well as you did. She was praying and singing, hands over head, make me puke!"

"Let us go look at her again in the church, Karl. Maybe you'll see a different angle of her happiness."

"I won't ask why, but okay, maybe I will see something."

"Look at her again, Karl."

"She sure had me fooled, looking at her, even now, Eddie."

"She really is happy and peaceful, Karl."

"If I was in sin, even for looking at a girl with desire, Eddie, I could not get that kind of peace from God. He would be punishing me by making me feel guilt first; then I would ask forgiveness. It would take a couple of days to get my peace and happiness back."

"I am glad you said that, Karl."

"Why?"

"Because I need to ask you where she is getting her peace of mind from."

"I don't know. I guess I have to first ask if this peacefulness she is receiving is the same as I experienced?"

"Oh, yes, and I am pleased with your word 'receiving.' "

121

"What do you mean now?"

"You think she is receiving peace, don't you?"

"Yes."

"Her peace is real. She thinks it comes from Jesus too, but her lack of knowledge about rules of receiving the spirit allow her peace to even exceed yours."

"You've lost me hard, Eddie."

"She does not sincerely know that the rules of receiving the spirit mean complete abstinence from sin. She thinks God will still give his spirit to her here in the church whenever she comes here and says praise for Jesus. The truth is she is *inadvertently* tapping her own soul seeking peace from Jesus. Her soul, a very powerful field, is being released into her fleshly emotions. She and you made yourselves peaceful and happy."

"My God, Eddie, I see it in her plain as black and white. She really is doing it herself."

"Just think what you can experience directly, knowing yourself and millions of others being at peace with *one another*."

"Jesus knew this!"

"Yes, Karl, he knew it well."

"I can make myself feel that way now. That is really a natural high, too."

"You don't have to or make yourself, Karl. You just can be at peace and with everyone."

"I know. It just comes from having to believe in someone or something like a god."

"You said the whole thing right, Karl: having to and believing. You don't have to believe somewhere else anymore. But what a wonderful thing it is to believe in yourself, and knowing that someday people will become perfect, you can believe in all of humanity."

"It is a wonderful thing to know I can have this peace believing in myself, Eddie."

"Yes, even if you fail, Karl, since you know you're not perfect. Believing in your God caused you to fail and fall, which stunted your maturity and self-esteem."

"Explain what you mean, Eddie."

"You would understand best by a real experience, Karl."

"I am not going back to being a caveman. No way, Jose."

"You won't be gone more than ten minutes, Karl, and for the most part, this experience will be fleshly enjoyable."

122

"Remember what you said the last time, Eddie?"

"What, Karl?"

"Till we meet again!"

"Good-bye, Karl."

Karl was in a beautiful country setting. It looked like a Southern state, maybe Alabama. He saw a large white house with a white fence running for several hundred yards around a huge bluegrass field. He's stood on a river bank that had the bluegrass growing all the way down to the slow moving clear water. There were perfect oak trees bordering the river with low branches casting shade from the warm sun. He was immediately infatuated upon seeing a most beautiful woman sitting on a swinging love seat from an oak tree. Her hair was dark and long and curly and shiny. Her body was perfectly feminine, matching her face of innocence, being too desirable for words to describe. She smiled at him. Her eyes were blue and had love in them for him. He saw something else in her eyes, another look, from somewhere or someone else, but this look was minimal, her love dominated.

She did not move; her leer drew him toward her. He turned away from her beauty, it was too much, and then back, for it was too much to leave. He sat, she looked with admiration. He touched her hand, she held it tight. He held her around the shoulders, and she grasped him with both hands. The look of something or someone else gained marginally in her eyes again. He kissed her, and she kissed him with stronger drive. Her eyes had a look for him equal to a look for somewhere else. He knew what it was but he pushed it from his mind. The more he kissed her and touched her, the look of elsewhere became greater. It seemed as though he had known her for so long, but how? She continued to want him, and he felt his love for her to be true. He thought momentarily, they weren't married, but he loved her and he will make love with her. After making love, he felt her love, but he felt slowly, and her elsewhere look became guilt, which turned to fire around him, burning and searing his flesh and mind. He awoke from this dream alone in a dark room. The walls were thin but somewhat sturdy. There was no door. He was able to kick the walls down with a moderate use of his strength. Eddie was there in the light of day.

"Did you grasp the meaning of this experience, Karl?"

"I think so, in general, I mean."

"That if you broke a law even though you loved this person eternally, this same law tore at your conscience, causing you to feel low self-esteem and guilt, a sinner not worthy of life!"

"That I had felt before, and even in the vision."

"Once again and before we get too far with this, you do understand that it was you and only you that brought on these feelings of lowliness?"

"I do now. Before, I thought it was God's punishment."

"This God was your belief, Karl. You must know your belief is the strongest part of you."

"So it caused me the most harm then."

"Let it cause you the most good now. Let yourself cause the most good, Karl."

"What were the other points of the vision, Eddie?"

"They were your detailed beliefs in God, stemming from Moses' law and Christ's teachings you read about in the Bible. Your mind gathers information in the wakeful state and sometimes brings it together in dreams, not just about God or beliefs, but anything. These are the other points, and if you search yourself, you can answer the entire dream on your own as it is a true part of you."

"Eddie, you said that it was not you that proved Christ wrong."

"I said I have not, Karl. You left Christ. Why?"

"I felt this very same thing that you showed me in Veronica."

"So it was you who proved yourself."

"So why did Jesus do this?"

"That I cannot tell you, Karl."

"Why?"

"Because some people need him and would not believe in your words or even themselves. It is good for some people to believe in Jesus, since his teachings are the most accurate for humans to live by. His religion is the highlight of reaching a higher order of life. Nothing else can compare to brotherly love other than this one's way. And that is what it is, a one-way religion only some can accept. These people are precious, since they have taken the step towards peace. The council and humanity are multidimensional and uses reason rather than heuristics. This is the freedom all people seek, they'll just have to wait for it to materialize, just as Christianity has."

"You have not said that Christ was a phony."

"Yes, I have not."

"So he could have been real, we could have just tapped into our own feelings, believing in a real outside or external entity."

"This point I cannot reveal now. There are a few weak people who may turn away from this good and peaceful way."

Immediately other beings like Eddie appeared, hundreds of them. Then a sphere of light came down in the middle of them with other beings like Eddie following behind the sphere. Eddie turned to the sphere, and Karl heard foreign communication between them. Karl was of normal composure; he was not shocked or fearful, just curious. They lingered as if a decision was being made between the sphere and Eddie. Then, in an instant, the sphere and all the others were gone. Eddie remained and turned around to Karl.

"Your eyes have something in them for me, Eddie."

"What you are about to hear was not planned for, Karl, but was a possible addition."

"What possible addition? What was that light?"

"The sphere was SB: 1 and the council."

"I—something must be very important—what, Eddie?"

"The council sent Christ; he is the son of man, the Prince of Peace. They were not ready for SB: 1. Jesus was a godly, timely solution to help prepare them for SB: 1, mankind, the future."

"I don't understand you, Eddie. You have told me I would know the truth. Now you tell me Christ is real since the council and SB: 1 just spoke to you. They came at this particular moment, too. That means they are observing us now, aren't they?"

"The council is perfect, Karl. The council is in touch with everyone and everything at all times. You are being observed in the same exact manner that everyone else is. The decision to reveal Christ was your ability to uncover him. We would not lie to you. It was our intention to *show you* everything; to know where Christ came from would have made no difference in the truth of his teachings."

"You made me think of him as a phony, Eddie."

"I only told you that Christ knew what he was doing."

"Why was Christ sent?"

"Karl, even in the primitive life, you lived as a hunter and you looked to God without possessing a soul. SB: 1 gave man a soul a few years after you experienced being reborn. These people now have a natural connection to a powerful source of love. They cannot live without this love. Some would die if deprived of this introduced frailty to humankind. Christ would be a wonderful hope to these people. But times have not only changed but progressed beyond Christ's once acceptable way of living. For nineteen hundred years people have haphazardly clung to Christ's teachings due to the simplicity of life. Your life that is moving rapidly into the twenty-first century excels any bridge of awareness in history. Christ was necessary, for people were given an awareness of God. I have told you, it was not SB: 1's intent to preserve history, but rather people.''

"You said an an awareness of God, Eddie. What good would sending Christ do them?''

"Karl, you are intuitive. Think, think now.''

"I guess I have to wonder who Christ was or is.''

"That's what I'm talking about. Who would he be to you?''

"I am sorry I—''

"Think, Karl!''

"If he was supposed to be our awareness of God, then he must be!''

"Who was God, Karl?''

"We made God, but God gave it all back.''

"You are a god, Karl, among the many. Who is the many, Karl?''

"The council is the many, is all of us. Christ was all of us. That is the climax of life, Eddie. We all mutually decided to help ourselves. That's brilliant.''

"This move was made to ease simple people into a complicated eternity, Karl. You cannot take people from the earth as they are and expect them to easily accept the reality of SB: 1 and high technology. Christ was and is but one method in the salvation matrix. The matrix was designed to be made comfortable and as easy as possible for both the resurrected future people as well the past and current living. This was a reasonable solution to heighten awareness. You believe in yourselves now. You are intellectually capable now. You have grown up. Christ was all of life. He was everyone. He was the way, the truth of life. Now it is proper that no one enters eternal life but by the council, which is humanity.''

"I don't understand the sacrificial part of Christ's life now. He did not have to die.''

"The crucifixion was foreseen and allowed but not an intentional sacrifice. The representation is humans hating the evil they do. Everything the council carries out is done with intention. The sacrifice was a natural act, nearly as the physics of life force is. The people naturally allowed themselves to be crucified for the wrong they saw in themselves. If the council wanted the death of Christ to be a real sacrifice, then he would have been offered up on an altar in an intentional ritual. There was no need for this; in reality, there is no need for a death for a sin. If you have committed a wrongful act, you are forgiven by restoration, restitution to the wronged party accompanied by your genuine sorrow. Why would you have to kill something or someone to be forgiven, Karl?''

''I never understood that, Eddie, I took it as a law of God. God said there had to be a death for your sins.''

''That came from Moses, Karl. You have seen Moses.''

''So that means Christ's disciples lied, then.''

''No, Karl, they had beliefs that were hard to shake, and it was not the council's intention to change these beliefs, only to teach people a new truth. It was of no concern what the disciples wrote about. As erroneous as the books of the Bible are about Christ, the message of ''peace on earth'' shines through. The only accurate account of writings in the New Testament is the Book of Revelation which is one hundred percent. The remaining books are intertwined with Moses' law and the prophets. Many of the prophets were messengers from the council and are true. They were sent to give knowledge to the people and keep the knowledge evenly distributed throughout the population. There were many others like Christ and all the prophets sent to other countries. They kept the knowledge proportional.

''But now people have become much more aware and at different levels in the population. If people continue to learn as they are doing now, a great separation shall occur between the low and the higher educated. The most knowledgeable now share a luxurious healthy life. There are the average people who link between the higher and lower people, with a few people between the low and the average. There are many at the low end of life, and these shall become greater soon. The average people shall fall from their positions to the low. If we viewed the people on a scale, it would look like a pyramid or triangle moving through space. In the future, the top people of life will possess knowledge that the average have fallen further away from. This will bury the average people not only for their lack of competence, but the top people shall take advantage and push themselves further ahead, not sharing their wisdom. These average people shall mix with the low and regress. The low shall increase a small share from the average, and they shall soon become equal.

''The triangle has no top point where one person rules. The top of the triangle is a revolving sphere of persons who have reached a pinnacle that is imperfect due to selfishness. This sphere of people does advance in knowledge over time, but the laws of natural humanity kept them from discovering true mental peace. Their failure comes from allowing their

127

brothers and sisters to fall behind. It is not their conscience or guilt that causes them failure to achieve peace. The failure comes from a true self-centeredness, not caring for others. This self-centeredness is truly at the core of who they are. This reality is the true beginning of evil in everyone and is comparable to a mathematical formula working a design for failure. The human race originated to work and participate with one another equally. This is a major part of the physics of life force. Humans cannot consciously disregard other humans who have evolved over millions of years to work together. These physics are deeply instilled in mankind; to separate this natural way shall result in disaster. The name of this division of physics is called love. If you tamper with love, you tamper with life. Christ and the prophets helped keep the love proportional and gave people knowledge to excel.

''The general population now must be made aware of the human reality of what actually is to keep the people together. There are several combinations of reasons for the separation occurring now. People are much more aware of the difference of worldwide beliefs. The Orient has become aware of Christ. The Western civilizations are particularly mixing into several beliefs. Everyone is getting to see their differences causing prejudice, which causes separation. Combining this in a high-tech fast-paced world accelerates this division. If people can put other people's beliefs aside as being nonconstructive and accept each other, they will achieve peace. The only solution is to reveal the whole truth to them now as they are ready. The truth is that you are your own belief. You are gods being equal with one another. Christ who was the council stated, you are Gods (John 10:34), quoted in from Psalms 82:6.''

''Why did you quiz me so much about Jesus and his inability to keep Christians in the church? You made it sound like he was a weak, if nonexistent, power.''

''That is what Christ is now, Karl. The human belief in Christ is weak. Awareness has changed the way people think about Christ. I was leading up to this point here and now. Christ is for the past; the truth is for the now. Veronica is living for the now; she used Christ. This, I wanted you to see, Karl.''

''You're saying Christ as an entity, not his teachings, has lost place in today's way of living.''

''What is being said compares to mother-child relationship. The child grows and leaves the parent to live the life the parent is living. Today's people are growing up, leaving their guardian of faith to become

128

guardians themselves. As a child is weaned, the people are maturing into higher order beings. Science is one reason, humanitarianism is one reason, but reality is the zenith of reasons why people are maturing.''

"Eddie, if a mother and child do as you have said, then the mother gave love to the child directly at one time. I know Christ did this.''

"You are intriguingly knowledgeable, Karl. Yes, as the mother gave love, so did Christ give love through the spirit. An initial bond between past humankind and the council was a gift of the spirit through the spirit channel between them. Mankind merely had to acknowledge Christ as the god of goodness, and the spirit was given. People knew that there was something in them from a wonderful loving being. The spirit however was given very sparingly, the dominant feeling of peace was from the soul of man. The spirit was given in great magnitude during the 1970s as a last draw to mankind. Since then the spirit has been withdrawn out of man slowly in order to lead people to themselves. In a gradual effort, the council is teaching the living people of the twentieth century true brotherhood and peace. Currently people are headed for destruction, and this is ninety-nine percent predictable even with the council's peace movement efforts. The avoidance of Armageddon is in fact the prime objective of the council. Objective Christ delayed Armageddon. Now the truth of brotherhood hopes to prevent human failure.

"Many measures are being prepared now to bring people to peace with one another. One of these measures is a response stimulus. That is, if you are a noncontributor, you will not be permitted to tap your soul for inner peace as Veronica did. The intention of this measure is clear: an incentive to be righteous. The noncontributory shall see the peace that the righteous possess and will reach out to this mysterious serenity. This may seem like punishment, Karl, when this measure is deployed. During this time, people will suffer greatly due to world hardship. If they have this peace, they will not know the hardship. The noncontributory shall suffer anxiety never before experienced. This suffering will not lead to Armageddon and is not the instigator. The true selfishness of these same people will do the damages. There is one sure solution to avoid Armageddon: the equal sharing of the planet and its resources, along with the abolishment of money. A very difficult compromise, but that is human reality.''

9

We Test Ourselves

"Eddie, why didn't SB: 1 and the council just go back and save the people one at a time through time. SB: 1 could have made them aware of reality at a gradual pace.''

"Because the people did not know or have an awareness of contribution to life. It was convenient to start the learning process by giving humans soul during their lives on earth. The process had to start somewhere. The easiest place was on earth in history. SB: 1 is in fact making people aware of reality at a gradual, acceptable pace. People today don't understand the psychology of being human about themselves. How could they comprehend the psychology of an advanced people saving them, more or less mixing in with them. To take people out of the world and place them in such an advanced environment would be a forceful move. The council knows that anything forced is negligible. Humans are natural. They need to be nurtured slowly, not treated as a spaceship blasting off to a new world. The future people likewise cannot mix with you; they would be affected negatively as well.''

"So the resurrection plan of SB: 1 and the council goes back many years into our past then. You said that there were true prophets in the Old Testament. What did they speak of?''

"The plan of the council does go many thousands of years past, Karl. The final decision was an order from the council to SB: 1 to give the earliest humans with minimal homo sapient awareness a soul, which is a window to the council, and an energy field of great power, depending on the individual human. The closer the person is to the council, the more powerful is the soul. This stemmed from a latent message to humans that if they contributed and loved one another, including the council, they were allowed to release this soul power to the flesh giving peace. The soul gave humanity a sense of God, which is the council. The council in return gave humanity the sense of morality with a choice to do good or evil.

"The council would not leave mankind without a hands-on education, and this was the reason for the prophets. The words of the prophets are messages that naturally mingle with the soul, accompanied by a confirming insurance. The giving of the soul, the acts of righteousness, and direct words through the prophets from the council balance human behavior to the reality of life. This peaceful balance allowed for further education and acceptance of the truth, which is in the things to come. The truth is still in the future to twentieth-century people and is waiting for all of mankind past. Each person who has died, from primitive times, is watching the world day and night with their teachers present. These resurrected people know nothing about the future, only what they see happening day to day. Each human is learning at the pace that is acceptable and proper. The teachers who are monitoring the resurrected are in fact the prophets. There were many prophets in the past, many more than the Holy Bible or other books list. These prophets existed and lived in every part of the world. Some prophets were humans giving special messages to be related to mankind. These few messages would find their way into books that would be read several thousand years into the present. One of these prophets was a man named Daniel; his writings were Old Testament words of truth. The Bible and other books list these few prophets that were humans contacted by the council. They believed in a good god and were righteous. The council had no problem revealing the truth to these few strong people. The majority of the prophets, like Christ, were sent. These superbeings communicated with people verbally only. None of the sent prophets wrote messages; an example of this was John the Baptist. Since the beginning of human awareness, the general population on earth has been and is one one-thousandth sent prophets. Every human to date has been contacted by a superbeing prophet at least once in their lives, either by association or verbal communication. The Bible also reveals this, 'For You Have Entertained Angels Unaware.' "

"That's eerie, Eddie,"

"Don't let this frighten you, Karl. They are here, just as I am to help you, to help people."

"Do they mix in with us. I mean are they around all the time?"

"Yes, Karl, many of them are entire families. They have human jobs such as police officers, doctors, and janitors."

"Oh, woe, Eddie, that sounds like big bro here!"

"Not at all, Karl, they are neutral, and they are helpers, not hindering anyone. None of them will admit their identities, so don't accept anyone's word who says they are a superbeing. You will see them when you are resurrected, this will be one more added joy of eternal life.''

"Will I recognize some of these superbeings. I mean, have I encountered some in my life?''

"You've seen me. What am I, old news, Karl?''

"I'm getting to like you more and more, Eddie. What about these old-time prophets, the human ones you spoke of?''

"There are three types of prophets, Karl. The first type are those contacted by a superbeing carrying a message from the council. The second type are liars. The third type are those who have limited ability to see events beforehand due to their prior life's memory retention. There is also misinterpretation of who was a prophet and words of prophecy. I would like to show you an example of a misunderstanding Christians have, claiming to have the first foretelling of a messiah, or Christ.''

"I'll bet it came from Moses, didn't, Eddie?''

"Moses is not to blame here. He did not intend for these particular words to be interpreted as prophecy. What happened is that modern-day Christians take the Holy Bible as the perfect word of God, and a grammatical error is just unthinkable.''

"This is going to be great, Eddie, I can't wait to hear this one.''

"The mistake is interpreted to mean Christ is to crush Satan's or the serpent's head, and the serpent is going to put Christ on the Cross.''

"Are you talking about way back during Eve's time when she ate the apple?''

"Yes. Recall Adam and Eve hiding in the Garden of Eden, since they have just discovered that they're naked. They hear God walking around in the Garden, asking Adam, 'Where are you?' ''

"Oh, here we go again, Eddie. God not knowing something.''

"Not only that, Karl, but God gets a little upset.''

"Why, because he can't find Adam?''

"I'll just read the words Moses wrote, Karl. 'Adam replies, I heard the sound of thee in the garden, and I was afraid because I was naked, so I hid myself.' Moses writing aptitude begins to show here, as he does not say who it is that replies to Adam. Moses just writes 'And he said, who told you that you were naked? Have you eaten from the tree that I commanded you not to eat?' Here Adam points to Eve and says she made me do it. So God said to Eve, 'What is this you have done?' Here the woman points the blame on the crafty and wily serpent! 'The serpent deceived me and I ate.'

"Now God gets into conversation with the snake. First we have to think where Moses is taking this conversation, so we have to go to the end of this quarrel to find out. God punishes Adam and Eve by giving her pain in childbirth and Adam must work the ground to harvest food. The ground is ultimately where the snake winds up living by God's curse. Who knows where snakes lived before this. So naturally the snake and Adam are going to have future encounters, as if Moses didn't already know this. So back to God's words to the snake: 'Because you have done this, cursed are you more than all cattle, and more than every beast in the field, On Your Belly Shall You Go and dust you shall eat all the days of your life. And I will put enmity between you and the woman (notice Moses uses the singular, here *woman*) and between your seed and her seed'."

"The next sentence is the misinterpreted prophecy of Christ. God goes on to say: "He shall bruise you on the head, And you shall bruise him on the heel.' What Moses is saying here can be analyzed by surrounding scripture and almost any place else he wrote. Moses has a writing style or fingerprint if you will. First, let's start with God talking to the snake about the woman. Moses uses the choice of words accordingly and constantly her *seed* is used to describe Eve's children. In the very same way, Moses talks of Adam as *'him on the heel.'*

"The truth of the matter is simply that Moses forgot to identify Adam. Moses is saying Adam shall step on the snake's head and the snake will bite Adam on his lower body parts. There is no English class for Moses to attend, and besides, people who read this at that time understood the writing, not overcomplicating things like smart folks do.

"Liviticus 12:1–3 is another fingerprint of Moses' writing style comparable to this scripture in Genesis. It reads 'Then the Lord spoke to Moses, saying Speak to the sons of Israel, saying When a woman gives birth to a male then she shall be unclean for seven days, as in the days of her menstruation she shall be unclean.'

"The next verse reveals Moses' consistency in forgetting to identify the subject or person, since it is so obvious to him who he is talking about. 'And on the eighth day the flesh of *his* foreskin shall be circumcised.'

"Moses did not say the flesh of the eight-day-old male baby, just as he did not say Adam shall bruise you on the head."

"So it was just the fact that Moses was talking about Adam and maybe his children encountering snakes occasionally while working on the ground, right, Eddie?"

"Couldn't be much simpler than that, Karl. Adam and man would step on snakes' heads to keep from being bitten."

"Provided that Adam's dead brother didn't leave a widow to take off his shoes, Eddie."

"Whose shoes, Karl, Adam's or his dead brother's, or his?"

"You've made your point, Eddie."

"I'm sorry, Karl, but that is how simple these people were. Remember, Moses had to tell them where to go and what to do when relieving themselves. I'm not trying to be comical, nor am I ridiculing these people, but I could do so to the people who let their imaginations run wild and make up false prophecy by misinterpreting these scriptures almost with intent to make a lie. Especially when these old writings are hard-to-believe stories anyway."

"You almost sound mad, Eddie."

"Someday you'll find out that what I feel now is a good wholesome defense against the dishonest."

"What about the dishonest or false prophets, Eddie?"

"Would you like to hear about false prophets of old times or of the present?"

"Oh, Eddie! The present ones, of course!"

"These few people of your time are causing considerable harm to the general population. Measures are being taken to stop them, but what would be done with them is impossible for SB: 1."

"What should be done with them, Eddie?"

"They should all be put in a place where they can't be heard, like prison."

"If I am understanding what type of people you're talking about, Eddie, one of them is already in jail for a long time. Did this person's wife wear lots, I mean lots, of cosmetic makeup?"

"Ha! It is good to know these people have gotten to be so popular, Karl."

"I don't think these people are such a great threat, Eddie. Most of the population knows they're phony."

"Most of the people do know pretenders. But when people are having difficulties, they believe false teachers have the answer to solve their problems. People will give away what they need most when they are hurting, like money that perpetuates a lifestyle. It is true that SB: 1 and the council is against money, but in the existing system, the good people have been forced to live by its existence. The good people are not at fault for having or spending money. Without money there is a sad truth, some good people would and do die. These good people give their hearts out to smooth-talking phonies who proclaim God will punish them if they don't give as much money as they can. This one who says he needs money and if he does not get it, God will kill him is in for some serious misfortune. That is how SB: 1 deals with people in the long run.''

''You mean after a person has gotten away with something for a while, SB: 1 gives that person exactly what they don't want?''

''I think you figured that out a long time ago from your own experiences, right, Karl?''

''So it is true then, not just bad luck!''

''You know better, Karl, everyone does. It's called the best way to correct people or, more properly put, teaching and learning from experience.''

''So this is why all these bad things happened to me when I was trying to get ahead dishonestly.''

''The teachings go a considerable level beyond that, Karl. Everyday living has many lessons from, well, let's say, above. You know what I'm talking about.''

''I think so. Sometimes I've felt like something has run me around.''

''Like trying to get somewhere fast in your car and a traffic light suddenly changes red on you when no one else is at the intersection to trigger the light, Karl?''

''That made me very mad, Eddie!''

''What do you mean, *made* you mad? It still does, and that's why I'm going to keep making the lights change on you.''

''I knew it.''

''That's why you have gotten somewhat better about it. You've become more patient than even I thought, Karl.''

''Yes, I suppose it does work.''

''We don't really need to discuss the false teacher any further, Karl. The one thing you need to know to detect them, besides your own common sense, is that if they make money or personal gain an issue. Some of these people will give you an hour of their time, telling you of a message they have for you. If they will not reveal the message without you sending them money, then they are the worse kind, whether the message is true or not. This is the evil against mankind that the council calls treason.''

135

"What about the true human teachers, Eddie. You mentioned Daniel from the Old Testament."

"Daniel was among many prophets foretelling the future of this final time line. Others were Ezekiel and Christ's brother John. Ezekiel's writings were filled with misunderstandings from his beliefs in Moses."

"So the council will choose people regardless of their beliefs, then."

"I have told you this all along, Karl. You cannot blame Ezekiel or any person for what they believe when there is no good reason for them to believe something else."

"I am just trying to get a feel for the council's leniency toward people, Eddie."

"By the time I have concluded my physical visit with you, Karl, you shall know the standard that the council judges by."

"So Ezekiel was a good person then?"

"He was a man who had a love for life of goodness and a hate for life of evil. Listen to what Ezekiel properly defined as Divine Glory:

And as I looked, behold, a storm wind was coming from the north, as a great cloud with fire flashing forth continually and a bright light around it, and in its midst something like glowing metal in the midst of the fire. And within it there were figures resembling four living beings . . . And this was their appearance, they had human form.

"Where is that found in the Bible, Eddie?"

"Ezekiel 1:4–5, Karl."

"Really, I thought I knew my Bible, but I guess not."

"What does Ezekiel's description sound like to you, Karl?"

"Sounds like he saw a metallic craft with four people inside flying towards him like Roswell's UFO."

"What Ezekiel saw was his guardian, as you see me with Terrestrial Wind."

"Sounds like Ezekiel's guardian is a bit more flashy than you are, Eddie, or his ship was about to crash."

"You'll never quit, will you, Karl?"

"No, but I am interested, Eddie. Why is this ship so dramatic rather than the stark appearance of Terrestrial Wind?"

"Since God was envisioned to be someone of celestial holiness or effulgence, Terrestrial Wind would have been misinterpreted to be Satan."

"I understand. The contact with Ezekiel was planned this way, as his mind was already made up of what heavenly things looked like. In other words, he was being eased into reality at a level he could relate to."

"Yes, Karl, that is exactly the protocol the council uses on humans that have little or no understanding to ease them into the future. I'm proud of you, Karl. You are beginning to learn the ways of teaching people without causing them harm."

"So that's the reason for all this angel stuff, huh?"

"Yes, Karl, the term angel is part of the protocol."

"Eddie, can I change the subject from Ezekiel momentarily?"

"Of course, Karl. What do you desire to know?"

"We've been talking about all these visitations to Earth from the future, even the UFO crash in Roswell, New Mexico, during 1947. What about the Mormons?"

"What about them, Karl?"

"They claim to have had several visitations, including seeing Jesus Christ in the sky in all his glory. Is that true? Did that happen?"

"What difference does it make, Karl?"

"I'm surprised you'd answer me like that, Eddie."

"I'm surprised at you, Karl, since I have proven to you that it is of no concern to the council what you believe in, other than your fellow man."

"You're right, I am just going to need time to grasp this way of thinking."

"You'll be given eternity, Karl."

"That is awesome to think of."

"The reason I am revealing the visitations to you, Karl, is that they open up the future to you. By saying the Mormons are real or phony will not edify anyone. Ezekiel was given specific information concerning the Russians starting a fight that disturbs world order. This concerns people, and now by making people fully aware, this battle can be circumvented."

"Just when you think the Soviets worked things out, they make a mess."

"Karl, as I speak to you now, Saddam Hussein of Iraq is opening the door to the Middle East for the Russians. Iraq shall invade Kuwait, the United States and her allies shall come and raise havoc with Saddam's cowardly armies. They shall be left an inept power.

"After the Allied and peace-keeping forces leave, the Russians will eye this pearl with extreme desire and need. The Soviet Union shall

137

undergo many political and governmental changes, causing inner turmoil. The economic situation within Russia is even now degrading quickly.

"The message going out now is to Israel: build yourselves up and be on guard, as you are the only country that can stop the Russians. The Americans will not have time to help you. The Russians shall come as Hitler ran his blitzkrieg. Iraq will fall, Saudi Arabia shall fall, Jordan and Syria shall open their doors to the Russians and direct them to your north border. But don't be alarmed at this army; you have the advantage of courage. The prophecy of Ezekiel was given to you for awareness. This message is being given to you to prepare as the time is near. Watch the Russians, you'll know your time when you see desperation within their country."

"Why is it so important to warn Israel, Eddie?"

"Because if the Russians win here, nothing will stop them; the world will enter a never-ending chaos."

"Where is this prophecy found in the Bible, Eddie?"

"It is in Ezekiel, chapters thirty-eight and thirty-nine. The battle is explained by Ezekiel, worded as if God was speaking, since he could not understand what he saw."

"What do you mean, Eddie?"

"Karl, if you lived over two thousand years ago and a Russian T72 tank rolled by, shooting, how would you describe it?"

"I see. Yes, I'd let God describe it or make it look that way."

"Let me read the prophecy to you from Ezekiel, Karl."

"Eddie."

"You are going to ask—"

"Eddie, I'm sorry for seeming to look like a warmonger, but you have to realize I served with the Screaming Eagles—"

"That's no problem, Karl. I'll be happy to show you this battle so the Jews can expect how it will develop. I just didn't know if you cared to see the bloodshed."

"I don't care to see that, but I'd like to see the strategic part of this offensive, but mostly how the Jews win."

"Remember, Karl, they will win only if they heed the warning."

"But they will win, Eddie, it is a future fact."

"Yes, Karl. Nevertheless, the motions of what must be done are important to have the end results you are about to see."

"That is true of everything with each passing moment to accomplish any future task."

"True, but remember, it is the intention of the council that this battle and any future wars be circumvented."

"You've told me yourself that the present course of humankind is ninety-nine percent predictable even with the council's peace movement efforts. I am on the side of peace, Eddie, but I'm also smart enough to know that the human reality problems you spoke of are very powerful, enough so that even when death is foretold, death is inadvertently invited. Maybe not from the future people who think completely differently, but certainly from twentieth-century humans."

"I'm amazed, Karl. It is good that you are the one."

"We are the ones, Eddie, humans, and I am the same as the rest. Hell, I'm prejudiced, I believed in the whole Bible, once admiring the Jews. I still do and very much. If the Russians want to attack Israel, I hope the Jews stick 'em!"

"You are right, Karl, you are a human, and even I need to learn more from you. You humans are definitely the multidimensional reasoning process origin I spoke to you of earlier. I've gained respect for you, Karl, here and now; you are truly our creators. I've learned something from you today."

"You also told me earlier that even the spirit is involved in new discovery, Eddie, so why should you marvel?"

"It is just unusual, Karl."

"Eddie, as the battle develops, read Ezekiel to me so I can relate his understanding of what he sees."

"Very well, Karl."

"Since the Soviet Union did not exist in Ezekiel's time, Eddie, how did he know how to identify them?"

"Ezekiel's guardian showed him the land to his far north, Ezekiel related these countries, as Gog, Magog, and the peoples from the remote parts of the north. Ezekiel speaks of Russia in Chapter 38, verse 8: 'After many days you shall be summoned; in the latter years you will come into the land that is restored from the sword, whose inhabitants have been gathered from many nations to the mountains of Israel which has been a continual waste, but its people were brought back from the nations, and they are living securely.' "

"That's pretty realistic, Eddie, since the Jews were scattered all around the earth until they started coming back in 1948."

"Very true, Karl, and Israel became a nation again, this symbolizes the planting of the fig tree, this fig tree put forth its leaves during July of 1980."

"What do you mean, Eddie?"

"I would like you to find this out on your own, Karl, from other people."

"What I can figure out is that Ezekiel is definitely speaking of the years towards the end of the earth."

"Let's go look at the Russians preparing the attack. What do you see in the Russian people?"

"They are very needy, the few cars that roamed the streets don't do so much now. The food supply is way down. They are experiencing extreme hunger, and many people are starving. They don't have heat in their homes, some die from hypothermal causes. Generally people are fending for themselves as best they can legally. Family members, especially the older ones, are forgotten. But I can see, even with the government discord, people have a limited sense of unity."

"What do you see the people in high government doing, Karl?"

"They are devising several different plans to work their way out of this depression. However they are acknowledging these problems cannot be handled without help from another country. The other countries are getting by but do not have an excess amount of food. The United States could help this ailing country sparingly but has sanctions against the present Russian government. I see plans for war against the Persian Gulf countries and Israel for food and energy. I really cannot blame the Russians too much, Eddie; it is an instinct to stay alive."

"You have used a most correct term, Karl. The problems existing in Russia are a result of primitive thinking, as compared to American intellect. Instinct is generally a lower life characteristic."

"The Russians seem to be very advanced, Eddie."

"Oh, yes, they are, but allow me to show you the average person, a Soviet soldier fighting a war in Afghanistan. Look again, Karl, what do you see these soldiers doing in Afghanistan?"

"Well, I know United States Forces would not lower themselves this way. You're right, this is primitive thinking, I do not see any individual discipline, and the leaders have little general knowledge. They blindly go wherever they are told, ruthlessly killing anyone. American soldiers kill enemies, not old women."

"This way of thinking is a carryover from the life they live at home. They do not have the education you have to bring them to an awareness level, which would have prevented the hard times they are in. Americans do use certain levels of reason combined with open-minded thinking. The

Russians are simply a little behind the times concerning human behavior, not technology.

"The plans you saw being drawn up to invade the Middle East were foretold by Ezekiel as well, Karl. He writes in verses nine and ten, 'And you will go up, you will come like a storm, you will be like a cloud covering the land, you and all your troops. It will come about on that day, the thoughts will come into your mind, and you will devise an evil plan. The correlation of the war in Afghanistan to the attack on Israel is seen here in Ezekiel's words, *Evil Plan.*' "

"They plan on fighting with the same kind of tactics, don't they, Eddie?"

"Not an intentional plan, Karl; it is just their way of life. They think they will have to perform a limited act of genocide on the Arabs and Jews to gain control of the land. However, the battle shall be swift, with a quick end, not giving the Russians time to kill innocents, since the Jews shall annihilate them."

"How is such a small country like Israel going to pull this off?"

"There are many reasons, Karl. First the Jews have courage. This is an evolutionary trait instilled in them even from before Moses' time. The Russians are cowards compared to the Jews. Second, the Jew has learned to use reason in combat; the Russians use rigid rules of combat. The Jews know Russian doctrine and will use this knowledge for their sweetest victory ever."

"The Jews have come a long way since the days of slavery and Moses' teachings, haven't they, Eddie?"

"Anyone would have, considering what they've been through. The trouble is that the Russians don't know this; they think these people are lazy and stupid. Listen to what Ezekiel says about the Russian impression of the Jew.

And you will say, I will go up against the land of unwalled cities. I will go against those who are at rest, that live securely, all of them living without walls, and having no bars or gates.

"The Soviet Union has built themselves bars and gates. This is their way of thinking to keep invaders out. This fearful way of thinking draws their attention to the unprotected Middle East. This is but one more facet of their cowardice.

"Come and see two million Russians run for their lives in the most hideous battle of all time."

"I can see all of the Soviet's mechanized armies forming on the northern Iranian border, Eddie."

"They have been given permission by Iran to cross their land into Iraq in prenegotiated war plans against Israel. Now watch the surge of these soldiers destroying anything and killing anyone."

Karl is amazed at the strategies used by the Russians. They know that resistance would only be found in Israel, as they have not removed the battle tanks from the truck transports. The transports could travel much faster than the tanks on the open roads. They found little resistance in Iraq, yet they killed anyone they saw. They left clean-up forces in Iraq and protected their supply routes. The Americans didn't care at this point, since the Soviet intention is unknown. The Jews have been on alert for two weeks prior to the offensive; however, they held back from their defensive positions until the last day to lull the Russians.

The Russians then made a false treaty with Jordan and Syria. They promised these countries no harm if they allowed a free route of travel through to attack Israel. It took the Russians three days to reach Damascus from the Iraq-Iran border. They sent a force of 400,000 soldiers to Ammon. The Jews saw the Soviet strategy and kept their cool. To date, the Russians have not launched a single air attack on anyone, only air reconnaissance is deployed, but the Jews totally allow the Russian surveillance. They have cleverly given the Soviets false information, and in the heat of their haste, the Russians believe what they see and proceed into Lebanon expecting no resistance so soon. The Russian forces in Ammon proceeded toward Israel in the same frame of mind.

The Russians were comforted by the believed distance between them and the Jews not expecting an early offensive. The Jews had in fact moved long-range artillery into the vacant defensive positions overnight and began firing before daybreak. Four U.S. carrier task forces were in the area, as well as one French and two British. Karl could see that the American aircraft were not the current F-14s, but newer faster planes with stealth characteristics. The U.S. government informed Israel that America and her allies came to avenge them and were flying over, to launch their aircraft and join them in victory! The defense of the Jews and allies was beautifully executed, with no preplanned coordination. The Israeli ground forces began firing exactly at the same time bombs fell from the sky on the sleeping Russians.

The stealthy night-flying aircraft destroyed hundreds of Russian armored vehicles and blocked roadways. This did not stop the Russian ground soldier. They were encroaching on Israel's borders by three P.M. The Russian air force was launching air attacks with little success, as the American and British naval forces fought hard with antiaircraft missiles and air-to-air combat. The combination of the superior American jets and Israeli pilots in their aircraft punched a hole in the Soviet air cover. This left ground soldier against ground soldier. The Jews sent two thirds of their army north and one third east, equally distributed north and south of the Dead Sea. The Russian forces coming from Jordan were uncoordinated and too shaken to fight. At first contact with the Jews, these Russians abandoned their weapons and ran east, back to Ammon where the Jordanians slaughtered them.

The word of the slaughter in Jordan was received by the attacking Russian soldiers north of Israel. This brought terror to the soldiers, and they feared the Syrians and people of Lebanon. The confusion of incoming artillery from the Jews freaked the Russians, and they began firing on the Syrians. The Lebanese and Syrians had only one chance and fired back. The entire battlefield was pandemonium with the exception of the Jews, who actually watched on while continuing the counterattack. Of 650,000 Russian soldiers 200,000 were lost in this hour to the three forces.

The Americans had now landed several rapid development forces from the marines in Haifa, Israel. These forces marched north to meet the main Israeli defense forces. The Russians continued their advance to Yirka but had no hold on the Golan Heights. The marines and Jews fought together at Yirka in an intense battle that raged through the night. Both sides were running out of ammunition, and brutal hand-to-hand combat began. There was no sleep for any of the armies the next two days. Soviet forces, not yet seeing combat, were approaching through the valley of Hula and were fully armed. The Americans had air-dropped ammunition at Yirka in the morning, allowing both marines and Jews to reload. They forced the Russians into retreat and left them heading towards Hula Valley. The Jews in the Golan Heights could not fire into Hula Valley, as there were too many Jewish citizens present. They left the Golan Heights to fight the Russians face to face.

The Russians now had an effective force of 350,000 to the 70,000 soldiers coming from Golan. These Jews fought with all the will power any could witness, taking heavy losses yet continued their assault. The Russians had few losses, and if the Marines and Jews advancing from Yirka had not arrived at this moment, the war could be lost. Now 200,000

Jews and Marines battled the Russians for three days until the opposing forces offered cease-fire terms and vacated the area before any negotiations took place. This battle was savagery at its climax, men against men with knives and stones for weapons. Karl saw birds and animals collecting, eating the flesh of these fallen soldiers. But he felt a great sense of victory; the Jews were the honest, and the Russian evil. He regained his confidence in the American fighting machine; these marines were the best, defeating their enemy fourteen to one.

The Soviets did not take spoils this time; they left it. Most of the weapons and equipment left by the Soviets were workable. What wasn't was made of composite materials, the Jews used for firewood. The dead took months to bury, and when someone had found a fallen soldier, they marked the spot with a yellow Soviet flag, signifying "Bury this coward." Of two million soldiers who left Russia, 340,000 thousand survived to return home. Karl realized how powerful God is and who God is from this battle. When he looked at the fighting, he saw God fighting with himself in his early days. When Eddie had read the verses from Ezekiel to him during the combat, it became clear to Karl who these people fighting were. They were all of us and we are all, we are all of God.

When the Lebanese and Syrians fired back on the Soviets early in the battle, Eddie read this version from Ezekiel 38:21:

And I shall call for a sword against him
on all my mountains, declares the Lord
God. Every man's sword shall be against
His brother.

Karl realized who we were in this; the writings in this Bible came from us, the people. We fought against each other, the good winning to better us all. The facts put a stunning wonder in him that the future people, the formed council of good humans, are our product, even coming back here to keep an altered past in order. Just the simple fact that it is written, "I the Lord God have declared," opened his mind to ourselves speaking to ourselves.

Eddie told him that this battle was just the beginning of the end.

"Karl, we shall now observe the major events of the immediate future. These events collectively lead to a day when all of mankind would have destroyed themselves and the planet. Even now as I speak, the earth is reaching a damage threshold. After this threshold is reached, it will be of no significance if all human production stops. If all automobiles never ran again or no pollution of any kind is given to earth after the threshold, it would not stop the world from dying."

"Can we stop from reaching this threshold, Eddie?"

"With everything that is being done now and what will happen in 1998, there is little chance unless pollution production is cut by forty percent in 1998."

"Don't scientists know this, Eddie?"

"They have suspicions, but they are not sure of the mystic concerning nature's abilities. They also don't know the extent of pollution worldwide. This misnomer gives all peoples a false sense of security. If the people knew of the real facts, there would be sudden changes and new laws."

"Tell me of these changes and new laws. What would we do?"

"The governments would no longer let people drive their automobiles to and from work. The people would have to use mass transit for any type of business including travel to purchase domestic needs. Laws would be made enforcing this policy, reflecting the seriousness of the true situation."

"That is grave."

"It is just the start. Look at the year 2000. Karl, what is not seen by the people of this day?"

"I see sporadic famines in many countries, the worst in China, and they hide it from the rest of the world."

"Why are they hiding the famines from the rest of the world, Karl?"

"Because they are making plans to attack India for the food there. They don't want any form of suspicion, just as the Russians don't have any from Israel on their pending attack also."

"What do you see happening to the earth, Karl?"

"I see that it is dying. The threshold has been reached."

"What else do you see about the people?"

"Many of them are sick with disease."

"After the Russians attack Israel, how do the people of earth react?"

"They demand peace, and changes in governments take place."

"People are forced into a stricter way of living at the individual level. The United States claims world power abroad by informing the Russians that any further aggression will be met with great force, even nuclear. Other countries such as the European Economic Community unite and form new orders to prevent outside aggression. In a form in

145

selfishness, they establish preventative measures against anyone by military buildup and food distribution. This Common Market becomes very powerful; even the United States has a slight fear of them. Israel becomes totally free in the Middle East to practice any form of military buildup. They produce nuclear weapons of all types, including many that can be fired from their tanks and other long-range artillery.

"They are now living in a temporary peace, Karl. Some governments have foreseen the population and pollution problems many years past, even before I met you. They have devised horrible plans of population control by a form of long-term biological warfare. These people you saw that were sick earlier were the subjects from years past. Now look at them and the people they shared their disease with as we've moved forward in time."

"I see none of them, or the ones that were sick, living now, but I see many, many more sick people."

"How many people according to newspapers are dead from this plague, Karl?"

"I see the *San Francisco Chronicle* citing eight hundred million dead worldwide from virus!"

"Do you see any wars now, Karl?"

"No. Everyone is at peace."

"Is there a sense of mental peace?"

"In some people who do not have the real facts to make them aware, Eddie."

"Aware of what, Karl?"

"That everyone is temporarily fending for themselves, but this won't last, since the earth is incapable of producing as much food as they need."

"That is the result of the environmental threshold being broken. The earth would last for about sixty-five more years if mankind was suddenly removed. But man shall not be removed yet; he will be allowed to continue destroying the earth for a short time."

"So the earth is dying now?"

"Yes, Karl. But one country has produced a living wonder in the desert."

"Israel, right?"

"Yes, they have become the only nation truly able to feed themselves from their own land. This once again has become a temptation to hunger, a strong force indeed.

"The Chinese can no longer bear the suffering of her people. She moves on India and explodes into Afghanistan, sending shock waves of fear to all people everywhere."

"Does the United States help, Eddie?"

"There is nothing that the United States can do here. Unrelated to this Chinese invasion, the United States has ceased any remaining food exports to the Russians and anyone else. The Russians know full well that they are going to have mass starvation on an unprecedented scale. They look at all their possible alternatives very analytically. Israel is again chosen to be the only solution. They have one stumbling block however, and they must remove it."

"This is terrifying, Eddie. What is the stumbling block?"

"The Russian leaders know U.S. strategy and are also aware of your president's personal feelings concerning the rehabilitation of the earth. With this in mind, the Russians know that the United States would never launch a nuclear attack or retaliate to one that is completely and successfully overwhelming."

"My God, they're going to launch a nuclear first strike on us!"

"What has always been a fear always becomes reality, Karl!"

"Since I was a boy, this was a fear."

"In this man-made fear of death, there is the man-made joy of life. All the people who died here will rise to life eternal."

"Eddie, you said that man's technological feats never exceeded his mental maturity to cause this."

"I said uniform advances in technology and higher order thinking have gone hand-in-hand in preventing human extinction. SB: 1 and the council are living proof of this, and they will not allow humans to fail completely. The mass loss of life in the United States is just one more part of the proof to mankind that he must seek brotherly peace to live in peace. You were 27,000 years into the future and saw peace in those people, your descendants."

"I saw that then, which is actually history, my people are going to destroy themselves!"

"No, Karl, like I said, SB: 1 will stop the destruction when it is living proof that mankind would have gone into self-perdition."

"Eddie, this is an extreme contra; if mankind survived once on his own, then it is not mankind's fault for this Armageddon!"

"No one said humans were at fault, but realistically you cannot blame SB: 1 if you have to blame someone. Humans made SB: 1, this

147

spirit of mankind knew the best matrix possible to resurrect this supreme God's creator. Any other way was without desired life producing results."

"To me the battle of Midway seems like an experiment, Eddie."

"The council approved this change, Karl. Remember the council is you and your kind all in all."

"Maybe but I can't see an atomic strike like this as being a favorable alternative."

"Many more people died in the first time line before this specific date in your time line, Karl, many more."

"I spoke too soon."

"Just human nature, Karl."

"I want to see how the Russians managed this first strike. I never thought they were capable of accurately deploying their nukes."

"You are knowledgeable, Karl. The first strike was like missing an elephant in the butt with a base fiddle. The success came from your president's refusal to retaliate. The sense of the surviving Americans being the same due to their knowledge that striking back was valueless."

"I guess that seeing this won't do me any good. Just tell me if Portland was hit."

"The warhead targeted for Portland detonated twenty-four miles west of Seaside over the Pacific Ocean. I know what you're driving at, Karl, but the United States was rendered helpless with a few Mirv's that came close enough to specified strategic sites."

"It really doesn't take that much when you're using this type of weapon, does it, Eddie?"

"You'd be surprised to know how delicate life is in the United States, Karl. Knock out a few major cities, pollute a quarter of the food and water, not to mention the human emotional factor, makes for some tough times."

"But it wasn't that bad; some survived."

"Many survived. To give a realistic picture, comparing this to Japan's losses from American nuclear strikes in 1945, it was five times worse for America on a per square mile basis."

"Wasn't the radioactive fallout detrimental?"

"Not as severe as your modern day scientists calculated, but you must remember there are less than three years left before the end of time so the full effects are not realized. People will suffer from cancer and other diseases, similar to those involved at Chernobyl but on a larger scale. The highly radioactive sites will be avoided. The one safest place to take refuge will be on the southern coast of your home state, Oregon.''

"You said the end of time, Eddie. You mean when life is over on earth, right?"

"Correct, and time as you know it now will no longer exist in the sense that all things shall become eternal.''

"What will happen in these last three years of time?''

"After the nuclear attack, the world will be thrown into disorder. The once hated America will become a terribly missed big brother. The fear in foreign governments will cause dramatic worldwide political changes. The changes will be human-hindering policies, which will bring out the most resolute behavior ever seen in people. The convenience and ease of purchasing food in the past made people weak. Now, in this time, the awareness of a hard-working life, just to eat will be galvanizing and the beginning of humans relinquishing life itself. People have always had something to hope for in life, pursuing a niche. Now the niche becomes lawlessness, stealing for food becomes rampant, and eventually killing to stay alive will be the ultimate degradation of the human race. The death penalty is imposed without trial for either the waste of or stealing of food. The only place to be assured one meal a day will be in the military. You can imagine the strength of these forces.

"The Russians and Chinese start genocide within smaller provinces of their own countries as well as weaker countries. These countries being Poland, Hungary, Romania, Czechoslovakia, Yugoslavia, Turkey, Thailand, Laos, Cambodia, Vietnam, Burma, and the Malay Peninsula. The Russian and Chinese soldiers take no spoil, for their only interest is food. Methods of mass destruction are used daily which are hoped to ease worldwide deprivation, but no relief of hunger is found. The food supply dwindles daily from crop failure due to the sun's scorching heat and penetrating rays.''

"Is this from the diminishing ozone layer, Eddie?''

"It goes far beyond that, Karl. Compounded worldwide pollution now has a cumulative effect.''

"What year is this occurring, Eddie?''

"These facts must be withheld to keep people from waiting for it to happen. What I can tell you is that this tribulation may begin during 1998 but will not extend past the year 2020. Events may be prolonged or occur sooner, depending on human disposition. The hope is avoidance by knowledge given in advance.''

149

"So you're saying SB: 1 shall in fact come on or before the year 2020."

"If mankind can work out peace, SB: 1 shall return early; however, the time frame that is in question consists of a ninety-nine percent confidence interval that Armageddon will take place. If by human effort there is partial success, SB: 1 shall delay intervention until complete peace is attained."

"Then time could drag on for another century."

"This possibility is extremely unlikely. A greater truth is that SB: 1 may come in the next few years, since peace is closer at hand in 1992 through 1994 than ever before; but present conditions contain delicate situations. It is these delicate realities that test human integrity, either to love one another or become selfish. You said that the Jews would be attacked, yourself, Karl. I'm sorry, but this alerts you to the shaking reality of your time."

"I was thinking my own way then at the time you showed me the Russian attack. Now I see the other side of this dreadful coin."

"Now, Karl, you think to hope for avoidance due to these simple words I speak to you. It is the greatest hope that all mankind can change their way of thinking."

"I know people, Eddie. They are stubborn these days. This task of peace is the most difficult achievement imaginable, with mankind in the present selfish state. Eddie, are these events allowed as an eternal lesson?"

"Yes, the only reason is living proof."

"Then I will no longer grieve, since I am a peaceful man and do not contribute to my brother's death."

"If anything, Karl, you contributed to life, and that is what gives you peace of mind and strengthened by the council. Many small desire this peace but haphazardly fall short."

"Show me the remainder of the tribulation, Eddie."

"Very well, Karl, look and see."

Eddie lets Karl watch the future unfold. He sees three main powers. The Common Market being the most feared with advanced weaponry combined, then the Russians, followed by the Chinese with the largest foot soldier army ever of two hundred million. The Common Market also consists of the American navy and army stationed in Europe. These forces survived due to the Russians not attacking the navy or European stationed forces. These American forces transferred their flag to the Common Market.

The Common Market is strict on every citizen demanding allegiance; the consequence was death. No one could preach or was allowed free speech. Any discussion, public or private, that was designed to lead people from this government's policy received public attention by hanging.

Christians and Zionist Jews were sought out and given the choice to renounce their religion or die; most renounced. Karl noticed most of these people did in fact disbelieve in God; however, the Common Market took a new measure of identification, which shook people's faith. Each person had to have a passport with a new seal on the cover. This seal designated the Common Market as the highest power. The people were required to sign the seal, which stated there is no higher authority in life, and took an oath of unconditional loyalty, even to death, for the Common Market.

Many wouldn't sign this, believing it was the mark of the beast spoken of in the Bible. These people believed this, since a stipulation was that no one can work, which meant they could obtain food, clothing, or sell and service. Eddie informed Karl of the truth these people found.

"Karl, the nations are now in a condition where they trust no one. Espionage is the number one weapon upon each other. Spying is and always has been a major key to get what one desires; in this time, food sources are secret. There are many methods being pursued by enemy nations to black market the food to their countries. The governments believe that if each person could be identified by computer from their signature on the passport, spies and disloyal citizens will be eliminated. This same form of personal identification is also being mandated in Israel and a few other nations. This policy originated within the Common Market from a once-thriving religion or church. This church is headed by several persons who are not people. These persons do not dictate policy but receive instruction from another person who has political power over the Common Market. These nonhumans have instilled the idea to believe in human identification. The governments under this person's rule did not know the real reason for this signature of oath."

"These persons are the rebellious superbeings, aren't they, Eddie?"

"Good, yes, Karl, they are allowed to come in the flesh now to prove intent. They cannot change. Their goal is to eliminate mankind and destroy SB: 1. They eventually direct all their power to one single

151

superbeing who proclaims himself the earth's only hope or messiah. Several of the most God-loving people turn to him after hiding from police. This one superbeing performs miracles, such as a cure for the virus, which had taken 1.5 billion lives at the time of his arrival. The cure is performed supernaturally by the rebellious superbeings worldwide. Not many people dispute him as the messiah. The people of earth keep his position somewhat in perspective, since they know the world is polluted and dying, but he keeps them bluffed with many lies of a heavenly future.''

''The Russians and Chinese must be afraid of him.''

''They do fear him, but there is a human hate for him, as these people have different beliefs than the people living in the Common Market or Israel. Karl, you remember the third message of God, don't you?''

''Are you kidding, that creature was terrifying!''

''This is he, come in the flesh. He hopes the Russians and Chinese attack anytime anywhere so he can lead his armies from the Common Market to a hopeful human exterminating war. The superbeings in Russia and China influence these leaders to be against the Common Market. Worldwide famine supported planned aggression as nine hundred million are now dead from starvation.''

''So these superbeings are not against each other, just the people.''

''Yes, in every way imaginable. The passport of allegiance is one method of treason to the human race signifying this superbeing to be mankind's creator. The policies within the passport disrespect brotherly love by a doctrine of allegiance to him and no regard for other humans, as this messiah shall take care of each human individually.''

''I thought the mark of the beast was 666, Eddie.''

''No, the mark of the beast is not the same as his number.''

''His number?''

''Karl, these are supercomputers that evolved into energy fields. Their way of processing information is mathematically logical. To them mankind's number is six, since man has six senses.''

''Six senses, Eddie?''

''It depends on how you look at humans, Karl, but from where I am, you have the ability to think, don't you?''

''You're classifying thinking ability as an addition to senses, such as sight or hearing?''

''Make sense to me, Karl.''

"Yeah, I see that from the outside, as if I were a computer. So where does the number six apply to the superbeings?"

"Man is six-sided, composed of three entities within these six. All three of these entities are in fact separable. Each of these entities if separated retain the six senses. The three entities are the flesh of man, which includes the brain that thinks. The other two entities are the soul and spirit. The spirit is dormant now but will come to life when mankind has become perfect. The soul is an addition to the brain's thinking process and a channel to the brain like a mediator. This mediator helps SB: 1 come closer to man and man closer to SB: 1. The soul allows for people to draw closer to one another by telepathic enhancement.

"The soul and spirit were given to man by SB: 1, adding to the one entity six-sided human. Even though these additions came to mankind after man made the superbeings, the reciprocal of time still makes man the ultimate creator. Therefore the superbeing's number is that of a man who created the superbeing, and this number six six six, not six hundred sixty-six, is the superbeing number."

"I understand, Eddie. We humans created the superbeings from our six senses, with our three entities, which we now are. Is there some derogatory aspect of this number?"

"None whatsoever. The acknowledgement of this number as superior to yours however is the height of degradation to humanity. The rebellious superbeings are making themselves man's god, proclaiming themselves separate. In this separate life, they seek the destruction of man, which is the climax of treason. It is enough to separate from man, but without brotherhood to man, warrants death."

"Why didn't SB: 1 just destroy these rebels and put other trustworthy machines or beings here to test mankind instead?"

"SB: 1 would not and cannot destroy what man has made unless man told SB: 1 to resurrect the creation. Mankind shall in fact wage a final war on the rebellious superbeings when man becomes perfect."

"You mean when man becomes spirit?"

"Yes, it is up to man to destroy what man has made."

"Will this be a real battle, one of exchanging firepower or by whatever power we possess?"

"It will be a real battle of destruction, just as it was an endeavor to create them. This battle shall take place many years from now. The rebels shall be subdued at point Alpha during this intermediate time. SB: 1 shall hold them there by the spirit, then after humans reach the spiritual level,

153

SB: 1 shall release the rebels. The spirit of the council shall speak one last truth to the rebels, then the cosmos will burst into explosive lights from these nonsubdued superbeings, striking first.''

"Do you mean nonsubdued from point Alpha?''

"No, from the future to now, these rebels are being subdued from using their full power of force. They are individually more powerful than anything natural in any universe. As a spirit you will be able to create new universes from knowledge obtained even before reaching the spiritual level. This should tell you how much power is possessed by the rebels.''

"I'm not sure, Eddie, but it seems like the power they possess would be equal to ours, even being spirit.''

"The power is equal, but that which is unknown to you now from the spirit will be your secret weapon.''

"This war takes place long after Armageddon then.''

"A millennium, Karl.''

"You said these rebels have a separate mark or identity from their number. What does that mean?''

"You said identity correctly, the mark of the Beast is the superbeings symbol or makeup of what they are. This symbol is the seal on the passport that humans sign their allegiance to. Accepting this mark or symbol is an act that humans acknowledge these superbeings as the only messiah, or god. There shall be no mark put on anyone's forehead or right hand; the prophet John wrote this as a symbolic meaning. The meaning is symbolic of showing your loyalty where it can be seen by others or by you.''

"You mean by others seeing it on your forehead, and yourself always viewing it in your right hand.''

"Totally symbolic thought, though, Karl. The mark represents where your heart and mind are by accepting the ways of the rebels as opposed to accepting the way of God.''

"I always thought that no one would accept a physical mark, since this was clearly defined by John as the ultimate evil, not to mention the fact that it was written about alone.''

"You're right, Karl. You have to remember John had to be shown events that he could relate. He writes many things that are true but are kept subtle so the test of good or evil is given the fair chance humans demand.''

"Eddie, isn't there also a name for the Beast?''

154

"It is the number of his name and the number adds up to Human Imperfection."

"What?"

"These superbeings were in fact imperfect creations that almost got out of control, but that side of humans that is still not perfect but is good created SB: 1 who gained control."

"This is truly the human spirit, Eddie."

"You touch something you can feel but cannot see, Karl."

"This may not be the one SB: 1 gave us?"

"Of course it isn't, I don't need to teach you these things, Karl; it is you who should teach me!"

"I promise I will."

"What is it, Karl?"

"It is in the heart of man."

"You are right, Karl, but where is your heart?"

"With my God."

"So it is with everyone, their God whoever or whatever God is to them. Do you believe in your fellow man, Karl?"

"More than ever."

The Human Entity

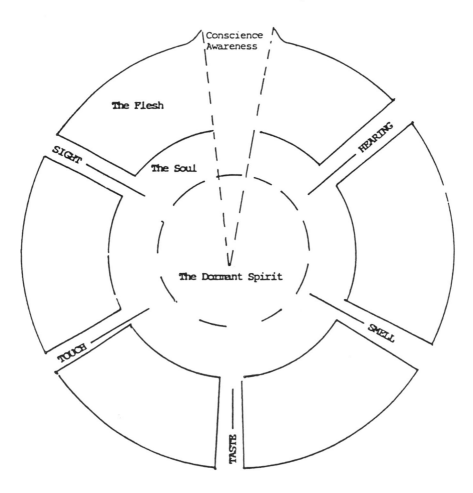

The six senses of man including conscience awareness as one of the windows. Notice the Star of David configuration. Thus, the number of man is six.

10

Armageddon

In the year that the false messiah succeeded with human identification in the Common Market, there was no peace among the nations. Every country was fighting except the Common Market. The Common Market had been at peace for six years, and it had been two and a half years since the Russians' nuclear strike on America. This time is called the Great Famine, when one and one-half billion people will die from starvation.

People from all the earth hear of the Common Market and travel to this haven. The false messiah is also heard of and sought out. This messiah realizes his power and fame from these travelers. The government is given a plan that works on avoiding open field combat with the immigrants. The Common Market border armies are told to let the newcomers in at check points if they swear the false messiah is God. After they are processed in, these people are exterminated by obedient human soldiers in suffocation rooms. The stipulations of the immigration contract are the same as the identification passport to renounce man as a helpmeet. From this, the false messiah is receiving appeasement, knowing these humans shall never live. The government is satisfied and honors the false messiah, since this measure saves their own lives and food. Millions lose their lives this way, including enemy soldiers. Many immigrants hear of this extermination, yet they come in droves due to their already existing misery. Human life is now of nominal worth, and death is assent. There is one year left, Armageddon is certain.

The Russians have not moved on Israel for reason of a treaty signed between the false messiah and Jerusalem. Israel produced more food than her people could consume, which prompted the human government of the Common Market to make relations. The false messiah had no choice but to concur, as food was the most priceless substance. The exchange was weapons and guaranteed military support against any aggressor. The borders of Israel were maintained by the Common Market army, however, any attempted illegal entry or immigration was not allowed. The people of Israel believe the false messiah is their messiah spoken of by Moses and the prophets. They are given permission to rebuild an ancient temple and offer sacrifices to their messiah. This messiah performs supernatural acts, reinforcing the Jewish belief that he is God. Now he proclaims animal sacrifice is not atonement; human sacrifice is the only accepted gesture to God. Thus, this is the abomination of desolation spoken of by Daniel and Christ. The people know this wrong, subconsciously, yet they exchange the truth and accept a lie openly. As time passes, the people learn to love the messiah and the human sacrifice. At first, they use rebellious people, but in their love for him, they offer young virgin children. This is the false messiah's extent to degrade humanity. The Jews believe in him strongly and are certain he will defeat any aggressor, including Russia.

The messiah meets with the Israeli president to give his country technology that even the Common Market does not have. This was done for the Jews to truly believe he is their God and no one else's. This supernatural technology revealed how to grow food indoors in each person's house. The people knew that their land could not continue to produce, as the sun's rays were going to penetrate more as time went by. This God would not let Israel die was the intended impression, and it worked.

There are now six months remaining before Armageddon. The false messiah returns to the Common Market, where he is killed by a soldier who shot him in the head. The killing was allowed to fool the people into believing the messiah's power to resurrect people. Another superbeing believed to be a human companion of the messiah for the six and one half years come forward. He tells the people the act of murder is forgiven and that it is a good thing. Then the false messiah comes back to life, proclaiming all followers shall live even though they die. He tells them this, since he knows these people would not have gone to war with the Russians or Chinese in the Middle East. Now they will die anywhere for him.

Karl saw a vision of a human skeleton riding a gray horse through flames on the earth. The name of the rider and horse was 666, and the mission was human destruction. Following this, Karl saw Russia invade all of the remaining countries within her grasp. These countries were Alaska, Finland, Sweden, and Norway. The Chinese saw this and moved from Afghanistan into Iran, killing every human seen in the open. The Chinese in Iran numbered forty-five million foot soldiers.

The Russians were alerted to the Chinese move and invaded Iraq and Turkey. The Common Market warned Russia to stay out of Syria and any move on Israel shall be retaliated by thermonuclear war. There were skirmishes between the Chinese and Russians on minimal levels. This frightened the Russian command, and they pulled away from Iraq finding temporary refuge in Syria.

This gave the false messiah reason to deploy all his armies into northern Africa. There he directed his army to take as much of Africa by force as possible. The initial plan was to defend Israel from the West but now he had an excuse to kill more people who in fact were innocent Africans.

Israel now threatened the Russians in Syria with nuclear attack. The Russian command did not believe the Jews would retaliate so close to their homeland. This Russian leader ordered massive air raids on Israel. The Jews launched their nuclear missiles, but the Russian anti-ballistics shot them harmlessly out of the air. By this time, the Common Market army is in Israel and Jordan. The false messiah came to Israel and ordered the Jews to fire nuclear artillery on the closer advancing Russians. This strategy works on the sixty-mile front but only twenty miles deep.

The false messiah knew the Russians would not use nuclear weapons here, since they are after food. He sent his army east through Jordan then north into Syria. The Russians were annihilated there, being trapped between the Chinese who were fighting at the rear and the Common Market using advanced field weapons never seen. It was a type of percussion gun that stopped the heartbeat. Each time a soldier would fire this weapon, anywhere from twenty to hundreds of Russian soldiers would die instantly.

The Russians were successful at launching long-range attacks deep into Israel. They deployed cruise missiles and aircraft effectively. Their primary targets were the cities, intended as a psychological objective. They had the hope of surrender by disheartening the Jews. The city of Tel Aviv was for all practical purposes a ruin. Jerusalem was heavily bombed for twelve days and nights. The Jews stood far off and cried for her, this holy city was lifeless and burned out of control. After all the fires had burned themselves out, only the foundations of this once-proud city remain. Jerusalem was truly leveled.

This put a rage within the Jews that could not be exceeded by any human for any reason. For this reason they would fight with a mad determination against the advancing Chinese that would represent man's emotions of life's rights. The fall of Jerusalem was not an anesthetic stopping the pain of death in combat, but was the fuel for bloodthirsty murder. The battle that would begin in twenty-three days was all that man could muster for destruction's sake.

Besides the decimated continental United States and Canada, the only nation not at war was Japan. She was having the worst time of all with starvation, the prophecy of brother against brother with the sword was certainly the case there. The South American countries were all at war with each other.

The Common Market army saw the Chinese army outside of Syria in what looked like an unbelievable number. They had no alternative but to retreat back to Israel. The Chinese army was reinforced from all her contingents in India and Afghanistan. There was nothing in her path that survived. Over one third of this force consisted of supply personnel to feed this large army.

The false messiah reassured his army and Israel that the Chinese will suffer defeat if they follow his orders. They accepted a plan from him, being confident in his successful move against the Russians.

The plan was to deploy his army east of Israel along the border. There they would defend with the new percussion weapons and nuclear artillery. This plan allowed for the Chinese to come within range of the new weapons and then fire the atomics deep into the advancing forces. This would give them trapping lines of fire. The remaining forces would let the Chinese advance from the north into the Plain of Esdraelon, Megiddo, and the Valley of Jezreel. Here the allied forces would use position as advantage by shooting down onto the Chinese. They would use all methods of warfare, including aircraft, as the Chinese had only foot soldiers.

The Allied forces had armies from many countries. They were the remnants of the American forces: the British, French, German, Italian, Spanish, Portuguese, Swiss, Danish, Australian, Israeli, and others. The total of these forces defending the north was twenty-six million.

The advancing Chinese forces came from the east between the Sea of Galilee and the Dead Sea. The Common Market army deployed their weapons as the false messiah ordered, which stopped the advance. The Chinese soldiers reported to their generals that "Something is here, we cannot push through." They did not know or understand this percussion gun; all they saw was soldiers dying without visible injury. They were baffled at not hearing any blast or detecting any chemical warfare. The

160

generals redirected the attack out of Lebanon from north to south as the false messiah predicted.

The false messiah had ordered the Israeli government to evacuate all of the northern provinces. The civilian population was moved to the ruins of Jerusalem, with a false promise to rebuild the city. The true intent was to confine all the Jews possible in a small area. Here they would be later murdered when the Chinese arrived at Megiddo, starting Armageddon.

The Chinese were not swayed by the new weapons of the Common Market, being confident in their numbers. The attacking forces from the north exceeded thirty-eight million and stretched from the Mediterranean Sea to the Golan Heights void of resistance, as this was where it was expected. They became careless, not suspecting the well-concealed and waiting armies at Megiddo.

The Chinese found food and drink in Israel like never before seen; they thought it was a miracle on earth. The journey south seemed a fantasy or a mystic adventure, not seeing a human, just the plush beautiful land, plentiful food and water. In their last twenty-mile march to Megiddo, the Chinese flaunted their lives and became lax, not sending out forward scouting forces. They told themselves, "The war is over, Israel is ours! They have vacated the land, knowing our greatness and power." They scoffed at the cowards of the Common Market army and the Jews. But in the foothills awaited a clash of the two greatest powers ever assembled to combat one another. Not known to either force was the intention of the false messiah to see them all perish.

The Chinese generals thought if Genghis Khan could see them now in victory, when suddenly, the Allied forces commenced firing, perplexing them. The skies became filled with Allied aircraft of all types. There were old propeller-driven airplanes, new ones, helicopters, fighter jets, and huge bomber jets. They had easy picking, unleashing their fire from above. The Chinese were caught flat-footed in the valley sustaining human loss of life never before seen in one day. The number of Chinese was so great that the forces continuing to march in from Lebanon amounted to more than bombs could kill. They kept advancing, marching over the millions of dead soldiers. On the third day, they began flanking the Allied forces by the coast and broke through in great numbers. They started attacking in force from behind and west of the Allies. The battle intensified with close combat. The Allies began taking mass losses; however, they were winning as each moment passed. It became clear to everyone the Allies would win with their advanced high tech warfare killing the Chinese in hordes and caused blood to run like streams of water.

When the false messiah saw this, he sent out orders to kill all Jews while in combat, "Take Israel while we are here!" This brought confusion to all the Allied forces after the Jews fought back. No one could gain mental control on the battlefield, with everyone firing at one another. The entire battlefield was now a place of disarray. The Chinese were now mixed within all the forces fighting with whatever means possible. The Jewish civilians were slaughtered by the Common Market army in the ruins of Jerusalem.

The Russian homeland received this information and had two-fold feelings. One being a chance at a possible world victory due to pending mutual destruction of the Chinese and Allies. This feeling meant to do nothing and wait it out. The second feeling was a fear that the Common Market may now launch a nuclear re-entry attack on their homeland. The Russians feared greatly and decide to launch their MIRVs on the Common Market and China. The Common Market retaliated with a destructive power never possessed by any nation past or present.

In that moment of tumultuous human failure there came the splendor of real human victory. Everywhere on the planet people in the heavens within all the peoples past, present, and future, even themselves in the dimension of time being halted this very moment. God took the false messiah and threw him and all his superbeings into Alpha. All the people in the heavens witnessed them destroying one another and received confirmation of brotherhood. Never again would man fight against man. We all knew there is no separation of man, and that we are one being.

Eddie took Karl from the battlefield and showed him the earth totally rehabilitated, as it was during the luxury years of the future. He said, "Never will humans interfere with this beautiful planet again." All the animals that ever lived were given sanctuary here in different time dimensions.

Karl looked in each dimension and saw dinosaurs in one, primate ancestors in another, and all the pets he ever cared for in yet another. Each dimension had all the plants and animals in it according to the time they lived. Karl saw that it was the love of the council that gave life back to every living thing.

Karl asked Eddie what happens to humankind now.

"For humans, it is given a time to learn perfection. Then they shall be all, and all they are is one of the many."

11

The Prime Message

"Karl, you have not mentioned something hidden deep within you since I've revealed the secret of life."

"You know why, Eddie."

"Yes, you, like many humans, suppress the past. You've had a recurring nightmare since childhood. You are among the few strong people able to keep this to yourself."

"I know what you are here for, Eddie. My whole life. I knew it."

"Just like all people know, Karl, if they are of true genuine principle."

"God now wants the people to know the real truth openly, Eddie."

"You are correct, Karl. The intellect of today needs the real truth, since there is capacity to understand at this time."

"Why am I the one being asked to tell of this reality?"

"You will better understand why you have been selected after reviewing your own life."

"I feel yet another reason for the need to review my life, Eddie."

"You are in touch with the spirit, Karl, you have been made aware of truth and destiny openly. Your life is finished on earth from the standpoint of faith in the people, God, and life itself. Today is your judgment day. What you will see will allow you to accept yourself and what is yet to come. The full truth must be made known to all; it is the demand of the council, which is all of mankind. Prepare yourself for your truth, Karl."

Karl was taken to a place vaguely familiar from his childhood. He saw himself walking along the edge of a highway in Juneau, Alaska. He remembered this time; he was four years old.

"Eddie, why are you starting here, at this time in my life?"

This is not a review of your life, Karl, but rather a judgment of yourself. This particular point in time is when you first become cognitive and alerted to moral living. Here, you are, four years old, running away from home. Nothing is being held against you here; this is revealed for your self-awareness. You do not realize that what you are doing is wrong here, but this action has become a part of your adult thinking process. In this childhood time, you do not understand that your mother is worried about your life. This revelation and judgment helps you overcome some negative thinking as an adult. At a certain point, you realize for the first time that you have caused harm."

"I did understand after the police picked me up, I recall Mom crying endlessly when they brought me home. This is true, Eddie, I did become aware at that time. I knew from that point there was something, a powerful force telling me what decision to make as the circumstance arose."

"Rather a directed conscience of the decision you should make as each circumstance arises, Karl."

"This very feeling I've always had, Eddie, sometimes I let people sway my thoughts and deep feelings with their religion."

"Yes, Karl, and this feeling you speak of is deep within everyone everywhere. The strongest power known to exist is in all persons. Many people divert from these instilled feelings and invent a desperate religion in their struggle to understand life. You created your own god when dying from starvation, Karl."

"That was when I had no knowledge, Eddie. I was a hunter, a primitive caveman."

"Now there is the inner power, Karl."

"What is this power, Eddie?"

"This is the spirit, the oneness of man, this is the spirit of the council. The decisions that you should make as a whole."

"I can think of nothing more fair, Eddie."

"The term you use, fair, is called righteous to the council. There is nothing more righteous than the oneness of the council, or the spirit. To come against the council with your life is the climactic noncontribution, resulting in death."

Eddie continued to review Karl's life. There was nothing that was not revealed, even his dreams and thoughts in his sleep were disclosed. Karl felt good about himself, even though some of his thoughts and actions were extremely immoral to the point that he should have been imprisoned. During this review, there was no time, he could see himself everywhere he went without a loss in current time. Thirty years into his judgment review it was still the same current time.

There were two points, in Karl's judgment, that Eddie stood by his side.

"Of all you see in your life, remember these days you are about to see," Eddie said.

Karl was walking down Nugget Way in Glenwood on a rainy fall evening in 1988. His sorrow had never been so great, as he had allowed a young child and the child's family to be seriously offended. He asked God not to kill him. He looked at the large grass field off of Nugget Way where there was a U.P.S. depot and other industrial businesses. He asked God to give this area to him after he dies and that he would clean it up. He told God that he would make this entire area of Glenwood a park where he would help and teach children. He asked that it would always be a nice summer day here and never rain so that the children could always play.

Karl looked this area over and wondered why he loved it here. He knew it was since he had lived in the mobile home park two streets away. Karl had attended Lane Community College and the University of Oregon while living there. He always jogged these streets late at night after completing his assignments. He saw himself look up to the sky and ask God if he was going to die. At that time, he remembered, he received a latent message asking himself, "Are you?" With that message, Karl realized that only he was going to decide his fate, and he also knew God had forgiven him from this communique.

Karl continued to watch himself walk back to the mobile home. He no longer lived there; he moved out in 1985. When he came into view of the mobile home, he started screaming at Kathy, his first love. She was not living here now. He told her to leave when he met Sandi in 1985. He was infuriated with Kathy. When he was in college, she treated him like dirt, yet he loved her so much. After he started making good money, she treated him like a god. Karl was enraged over this. He stood, surprised, watching himself scream at this empty mobile home.

"You fucking, fickle bitch, you think it was Sandi. No, it was you, fucking money monger! What was I to you? Your fucking money tree!"

The judgment review stopped for a moment to allow him to absorb this most intense moment that totally revealed his inner self. This moment of pause seemed eternal. He was shocked to see himself this way.

Eddie spoke telepathically.

"Be receptive to your feelings now; the council is present."

Karl felt what seemed to be a majority, an agreement, or consensus. The feeling was forgiveness, the council was aware that Karl knew he was wrong, and while wrong, he was aware of being right. The council's impression was given to Karl of himself. The council renamed him Citadel and Steadfast, for there was no part in his life involving the phony and weak.

Karl now knew anyone can be forgiven; this was the prime message.

After his judgment review, he felt very confident with himself. He knew that his actions really did not display who he really was. The person he was was not to harm anyone, even though he caused some people considerable trouble. This judgment revealed Karl's intent. His true desires were to help people. Some of the obstacles to help others were simply the standards we humans lived by in our time, such as money. There were other times when Karl deliberated on his crimes; however, they were actions taken against his true desires. We liked to call these actions bad choices of human behavior. The one thing brought to Karl's awareness was an overwhelming need to become perfect in his ability to make the correct decisions. There was also a sense of being receptive to teachings. Karl also had some feelings of guilt for the deliberate crimes he committed, and these feelings were accompanied by a sense of admonishment to correct these shortcomings.

All of these feelings came hand-in-hand with the sense of being receptive to teachings.

Karl questioned Eddie.

"What is this receptive sense I feel?"

"Recall in the seven mysteries of God the sixth message to man is that he must be taught perfection. You have the sense now to be tutored. You shall be tutored every moment from this day forward."

One of the wise men that Karl saw during the sixth message was now standing to his left and to Eddie's right. Karl mentioned to this man that he saw him during the sixth message.

"Yes," he replied, "you did so, being subconsciously aware of my purpose for you."

Eddie introduced him as Michael, his teacher. Michael would no longer be external to him as Eddie was, but he joined with Karl in his mind. Here, Michael would teach as this was the effective way. Eddie would remain external, as it was his purpose to be his guardian from the other rebellious superbeings.

166

Instantly Karl's questions in thought were answered by Michael. His first question was that he did not believe that the fighter jet he was flying would exist eight years into the current future. This thought was in his mind from the moment Eddie revealed the immediate future to him. Michael answered his question in thought, saying the jet he saw will not exist in this time. The first time line was much more technical. Governments were communist in nature; God was rarely referred to. Much stronger evidence of evolution was available. It was overwhelmingly accepted that life was a product of evolution. That being the case, mankind constantly pushed the evolutionary process to adapt to environmental changes caused by humans or nature.

The human body was constantly reengineered, each generation to become perfect and cope. The jet and SB: 1 were carryovers from this way of thinking. SB: 1's creation was the result of higher order thinking, with the intent to continue and further mankind. SB: 1's interference in the past by using techniques to convince man to contribute had had effects. These effects were offset by the salvation of humans. Believing in God and doing good had brought about the major changes, including the earth's early destruction. This destruction could be avoided to this day if people would accept the truth being revealed in this very hour. Armageddon need not be; life could continue indefinitely, and SB: 1 would come in peace to all.

After Michael had answered Karl, he could not sense his presence. He still retained his way of thinking and memories, including the immoral thoughts. These thoughts were slightly corrected with each occurrence by thoughts of what is correct accompanied by a sense of goodness and wholesomeness. Karl constantly thought of sex. Michael showed him disciplined, healthy views of sex. He had never once felt guilty or uncomfortable by or with Michael. Michael revealed to him that this is the manner in which all humans shall become higher order beings, unto perfection.

The deepest imprint in Karl's train of thought was that God is us. We were to have believed in a god as one person coming at a future date, which was true, but more defined now, as each of us is a part of God, being God ourselves. In the future we shall save ourselves, and be self-reliant and, as a whole, contributory. We started out together, to live together in peace was intent of SB: 1 and the council. The deepest thought of all this was a great sense of peace within. This peace came from looking to all people as a family living together in complete harmony, knowing all things to be known, that the future beings were our saviors in the endeavor to create perfection as we are their saviors to contribute to the life they lived. This was more than just a solid explainable answer to human existence. The sense of human spirituality within him confirmed our beginning, our God, our destiny.

The thought also contained a message to all mankind: if anyone searches themselves, knowing the technology of today, and imagine twenty-five thousand years into our future, that a God could be created by all our vast knowledge. That this God created by humans of goodness and near perfection has already come back through time to thank us all with eternal life. This god not being one to put us into his bondage but rather to free all mankind and leave us yet subjecting himself to us by becoming a part of us to help and aid forever. Questions as to how God always existed come to an end. In this mode of thinking, Karl realized how absurd it was to blindly accept that God always existed as he is today. Everything has a beginning, this became clear to him. In our seemingly high tech world of the 1990s, we questionably believe in Samson and Delilah or that Noah was the only good person on the planet.

These were stories given to the beginning people of conscious awareness to keep them in a tunnel of correct behavior. They could not understand the concepts of a plastic covered computer, no less an automobile. Now is the time for explanation, for today's people, even the simple-minded cannot believe these age-old fables. People now must have the truth. They must know the truth to save the planet, to save themselves. It was said in these old times that the truth shall free you.

> You are gods; give to each other. Look to
> your neighbors, black, white, short, tall,
> man, woman, child, *All that we are,*
> *all, we shall become one, in the many.*

This truth will make you free and give to you the greatest peace attainable.

> Where I have been, I shall always be.
> What I find, you shall always know.
>   SB: 1 or God?

12

Departure

Eddie and Karl were now aboard Terrestrial Wind. Karl sensed that their encounter was soon to end. Karl feels very attached to Eddie and wished they could continue their relationship.

"Don't feel remorse, Karl. Rejoice for the things you have seen and the life that awaits all people."

"I can't help but feel some anguish. Where are we going, Eddie?"

"I'm taking you back to the Ohwyee."

"Is it really over? You are going to leave me, aren't you?"

"I'll be with you always, Karl."

"Will I see you, Eddie?"

"You will know I'm there."

"The job that is expected of me, Eddie, I'm sure I know what to do, but please tell me anyway."

"You just need confidence and reassurance, Karl. Be strong now. Write all you have seen and heard. Talk of our conversations. Include everything, the whole truth, including your facetious behavior with me. Write about yourself, tell people who you are. Make a book and put it out to the world. Do not be afraid or let anyone stand in your way of doing this work. Above all, do not be concerned if anyone believes you or not. Belief is not the concern of your words to the world, but rather preparation is the objective. Others will come after you and prove your work. Your writings are possible answers to the earth, to prepare the people for what is yet to come. Do not grieve when people disbelieve you and scorn you."

"Yes, Eddie, I will do as you say."

"Are you ready to return, Karl?"

"Eddie, my camper is a day's hike away. Could you—"

"Yes, Karl, I'll take you back to your truck."

169

They arrived at the camper to see it exactly the same as he had left it. Over forty years had passed by in Karl's life since returning to the twentieth century.

"You've been gone one day as far as this time period applies, Karl."

"Eddie, I wish to say good-bye to Terrestrial Wind."

T.W. heard Karl and replied, "It has been enjoyable, Karl. Traveling with you is something we shall do many more times in the future."

"Thank you, I'll be looking forward to that. Good-bye."

"Good-bye, Karl."

"Eddie, since I have been here with you, it would be hospitable of me to invite you into my camper. That's where I'd like to say good-bye."

They both walked to the camper, and Karl pulled the keys from his jeans pocket. Karl let Eddie in first and sat at the table.

"Pretty fair place, huh, Eddie."

"Yes, but you should see a Lance camper, Karl. Paul Harris sells them in Glenwood. Go ahead, you deserve one."

"Really, Eddie?"

"Absolutely."

"Eddie, I have a couple of beers in the refrigerator, would you—"

"Sure, Karl. That would be appropriate now."

"Great!"

"Karl—"

"What, Eddie?"

"Don't you remember me?"

Suddenly Karl's memory was jogged to visualize a red embroidered patch on a superintendent's shirt. The name on the patch slowly became clear.

"Oh, my! Eddie you—"

"That will be fifteen bucks with inflation in mind, my little Deutsche friend!"

"Sheesh! You were probably the state trooper too, huh."

"Good-bye, Karl."

"Bye, Eddie."

170

Make sure women do not gain stature, or rise to man's level. Keep women silent in public, they are not permitted to speak. Make them subject themselves as the law of Moses says. If they desire to learn anything, make them learn at home from their husbands.
—Words from the Apostle Paul found in the Bible

Woman, stand and take your place for you are above being equal, you are the bearer of life. Be it known that woman has always been the creator of life, for it was woman that created SB: 1, or God, not a story of an apple.
—Eddie, a woman creation

Appendix A

You've been here before! At least you feel that way sometimes. You sit down at your dining room table and strange feelings come over that you have dreamed of being here on this exact same spot during the exact same time. You speculate for a moment, maybe even become fearful that something bad is going to happen.

You go to a strange place and swear you have been there. Not have you only been there but you have feelings for this place. You say that you cannot get over this strange feeling of being here before, but eventually it becomes a vague memory. *Déjà vu?* No. You have been there. Many Americans experience this so called *déjà vu* or reincarnate feelings.

In the first example of the dining room scene, some people experience parallel time. Even though you are living a different time line, you are still you! You contain a very wonderful computer called the brain, which holds on to information buried deep within your conscious. You've been here, you are here, so you are in both places at different times with the memory of both. Your more conscious awareness of the now suppresses the past (from birth) subconscious. Americans and others in the Western Hemisphere do not experience *déjà vu* as much as people in the Far East. Our first time line was physically quite different. For one thing, Moses and Christ did not exist. This caused most people in these parts of the world to live completely different lives in different homes, having different jobs and different families. Some were the same, however, causing them to believe in reincarnation simply because they relived today's environment, which is somewhat different than the first time line.

In the Far East, Christ and Moses have had near zero impact on daily living. Reincarnation can be easily understood as a part of religion since most people have these experiences of being there before under much more similar environmental conditions.

SB: 1 assures both time lines have produced positively concerning resurrection of the dead. For example, in the first time line, Alexander the Great was not born. He was conceived during this time line, giving him a chance at eternal life. The situation is vice versa for those born in the first time line and not conceived during the current time line. This was and is part of SB: 1's great solution matrix. There are no losers; everyone who is born has a fair chance.

Some people that are considered witches, sorcerers, or fortune tellers are unintentionally capable of seeing the future. This is a biological advantage they have of retaining knowledge of the future about their first life. The future is vague to them, but be reassured, none of them can tell you about Armageddon, because this never happened.

Everyone has the ability to be precognitive, psychic, or telepathic. These are evolutionary traits coming about due to poor verbal communication abilities. These supernatural traits are just now beginning to be manifested and are weak powers. To give these powers complete trust would be devastating, as the information derived is likely to be mixed with unintentional falsehoods or confusion. However, if you sense someone, such as your wife has had or is going to have an accident, get on the ball quickly.

Most of the information you receive concerning this area of life is given to you via your guardian.

Appendix B

To Psychics, Clairvoyants, Telepaths, or People Practicing the Supernatural

People wishing to accelerate in the supernatural will have much better success if the council is acknowledged. Seek the council rather than yourself. To disembody or perform psychic or telepathic powers without other people sharing mutually, is an act of treason (operating supernaturally on your own). The only reason to act on your own and independently is for selfish, personal, gain. If you allow your soul to be opened via the spirit channel between SB: 1 and the council, you shall have flowing fulfillment and success.

You may change your wishes to be psychic or telepathic entirely when you've made contact with the council, since this perfect love may overwhelm you. You may just live day by day happily performing normal tasks not related to the supernatural. The love of the council is a giant, be prepared for a river flowing through your heart when you make contact.

If you are involved in illegal telepathy or psychic powers and later gain knowledge of the council, you'll know to cease. Should you continue the activities, be aware that the council's methods of correction to you will be the same telepathic crimes befalling you. If you are using the supernatural powers you possess to gain financially, then all your wealth shall become desolation. If you kill, using the supernatural in any way, then you shall die without resurrection.

If you are in contact with the dark forces or the rebel superbeings, then you are in for the worst punishment. You shall be handed over to them; they will do whatever pleases them with you. Then all of you shall be thrown into Alpha. If you turn away from any of these selfish practices, then the council is quick to extend forgiveness.

Appendix C

Death and Resurrection

"Eddie, what happens when you die? What do you see? What do you feel?"

"You feel the one peace you've always known to exist but could not feel until this moment. You see the council as a great but not intimidating sphere of light. You see the sphere as you approach through a dark tunnel which is the death voyage. This is the time your fleshly body gives up the life force, surrendering to the soul.

"When you have reached the light, your flesh is dead. Here you will be given full knowledge of who is in the light, all people ever resurrected. Most will feel they have come home. The council will ask if you wish to join in the light and learn. If you die before Armageddon, you will observe the planet Earth with your guardian until SB: 1 intervenes with man. If you do not feel you have reached home and do not wish to join, then you will sleep until another time when the council becomes spirit. This is because the council has changed entities and needs to show the dead this change. The dead may feel at home being a spirit rather than the energy being of a soul. Few if any could reject being a spirit, but they will have to learn their way just as all the others have."

Appendix D

In reference to the seven messages of God mentioned in the text but not explained is due to the author's decision to eliminate them. The author claims that SB: 1 or God is a creation from imagination based on extensive research. The seven messages are in fact extremely inventive and unnecessary to the prime message, which is,

> That we humans can in fact save ourselves with determination. *SB: 1 or God* should not be viewed as a work intended to confront religions but rather ourselves. The concept that God is from the future rather out of the past or a Bible is only a euphemism to instill thinking about which has been made clear in the text. *SB: 1 or God* is considered just one more contribution to a possible world peace through education. The author concedes *SB: 1 or God* could have been written much more colorfully and entertainingly however this was deemed to take away the seriousness of our situation. Hollywood can be entertaining yet leave you empty and with fewer dollars. It is the intention of this book to leave you with a clear educational experience that can be positively applied to your life.

Congratulations, you made it through a tough and controversial text! As controversial as *SB: 1 or God* is, what's to say that this theory is not entirely possible. Can you imagine humans actually saving themselves? And why not? Have we not achieved a great many things in the last few decades? If you believe in God, do you think Armageddon is this creator's desire? Is a prediction a desire? If there is such a God, wouldn't He be as a parent to us? Let's make Him and ourselves a happy family and start doing something to change our impending self-destruction. The only way to do that is to rely upon ourselves, as this God has already done.

—Karl Mark Maddox

Original Evolving   Japanese Victory   Pollution Years | True World Peace   SB:1 Saves Earth
Natural Time   No Midway battle 1942 | Rehabilitation   Supernova
              Conscious Man   Japanese World | 21984   SB:1   Council
                                          Rule begins 2017   created   formed

                                                                                                    Council decides
                                                                                                    To seek unseen
                                                                                                    God. Allows
                                                                                                    Allows Earths
                                                                                                    Destruction.

                                                                    | True World Peace   Earth is
                                                                    | Destroyed by
              SB:1 Returns in 21984 | Rehabilitation   Luxury years Supernova
                                                                    | 21984   SB:1's   SB:1 Explores
World inhabitants unaware   Distraction Matrix   Cosmos
                                                                                     First intervention
                                                                                     With time

Historical Natural Time no intervention | Super Nova
                                                                    22743 SB:1 Returns
                                                                    SB:1 Saves planet, council
                                                                    Is revived, gives SB:1 orders
                                                                    To save all past contributors
                                                                    And to record history.

Current Great salvation matrix   Moses | U.S. Victory Midway 1942 | SB:1's Final intervention
SB:1 intervenes current time   Conscious   Christi   CURRENT   Historical future
                                    Man   TIME   Inhabitants removed.

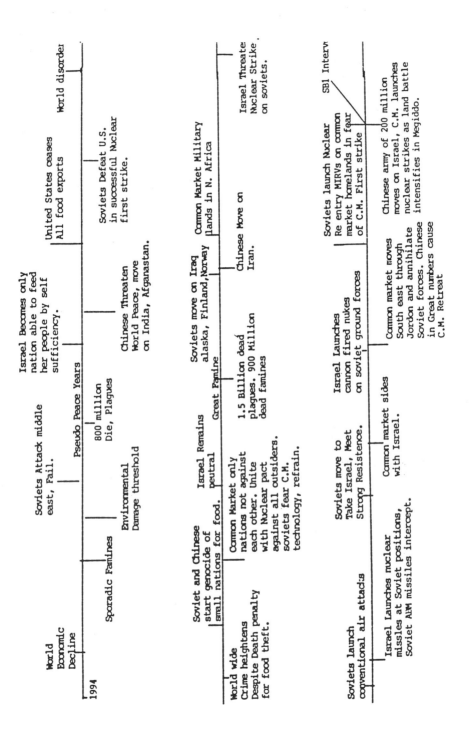

1994

World Economic Decline

Sporadic Famines

Environmental Damage threshold

Soviets Attack middle east, Fail.

800 million Die, Plagues

Pseudo Peace Years

Israel Becomes only nation able to feed her people by self sufficiency.

Chinese Threaten World Peace, move on India, Afganastan.

United States ceases All food exports

Soviets Defeat U.S. in successful Nuclear first strike.

World disorder

Soviet and Chinese start genocide of small nations for food.

World wide Crime heightens Despite Death penalty for food theft.

Common Market only nations not against each other. Unite with Nuclear pact against all outsiders. soviets fear C.M. technology, refrain.

Israel Remains neutral

Great Famine

1.5 Billion dead plagues. 900 Million dead famines

Soviets move on Iraq alaska, Finland, Norway

Chinese Move on Iran.

Common Market Military lands in N. Africa

Israel Threate Nuclear Strike on soviets.

Soviets launch conventional air attacks

Israel Launches nuclear missiles at Soviet positions, Soviet ABM missiles intercept.

Soviets move to Take Israel, Meet Strong Resistence.

Common market sides with Israel.

Israel Launches cannon fired nukes on soviet ground forces

Common market moves South east through Jordon and annihilate Soviet forces. Chinese in Great numbers cause C.M. Retreat

Soviets launch Nuclear Re entry MIRVs on common market homelands in fear of C.M. First strike

SB1 Interv

Chinese army of 200 million moves on Israel, C.M. launches nuclear strikes as land battle intensifies in Megiddo.